AFTER HAPPY EVER AFTER

WEIRD TRAVEL SERIES
BOOK 4

ADAM FLETCHER

WANDERLUST WORDS

It's nice that you're here. Welcome.

To be here, you've probably read another of the books in this series and that's great. This one is going to be a bit different...

This is not primarily a travel memoir. Travel is about escape and if anything, this book is about restriction: biological, political, geographical, or self-imposed because of how we see ourselves and view the world.

Accordingly, it's a little heavy in places, because life is heavy in places. It's light in others, because life is well... you get the idea.

It's based on a true story. I've changed all names and several other identifying details for reasons that will become obvious.

This is a story about strangers trying to becoming something else. A story about what follows Happy Ever After.

Let's begin...

To Stef, whose timely advice saved this book.

1

If some days are diamonds and others are rocks, yesterday dazzled, and today, not even an hour old, already had a hell of a shine to it.

I tipped my head back and closed my eyes, basking in the late-morning sun at my new love-interest's, Evelyn's, kitchen window.

It was another glorious day we'd pass in hot pursuit of each other. Twenty-four more hours of *me, her, we, us, yes,* and *let's.*

Outside the window, pretty little birds sang pretty little songs. I didn't know the words, but the sentiment was clear: *fuck me,* they were singing.

How late had we stayed up doing just that, pausing only to gush the stories of our lives at each other?

I didn't know.

I didn't care.

I didn't need sleep anymore; I was powered by her now. Or by her desire for me.

I turned from the window towards the stove. She was singing as she stirred what would become an African stew.

"NOOOOOOOOOO SCRUUUUUBS," she sang,

banging the ladle against the side of the pot, then speeding up. "Don't want no scrubs!"

Was I a scrub? I wondered.

I didn't have a job, in any normal sense. I was a writer, mostly, sometimes. Not one that owned a car. In fact, I couldn't even hang out the passenger side of my best friends' rides, since none of them had cars either; Berlin was a city of bikes.

"I love that you love to cook," I said to distract myself from myself.

She turned and grinned. "I love that you love to eat."

I kept watching. I watched her often: as she brushed that vast cloud of golden-yellow hair; or standing in front of her full-length mirror, pirouetting while nibbling the edges of her lip, comparing outfits against her mood; or furiously tapping at her keyboard, trying to right political wrongs. I loved the regalness with which she moved, and that permanent, slight surprise on her top lip as if she'd just been transported here from a 1950's movie set in which she was the bunny-dipping starlet.

I walked over and wrapped my arms around her waist. She tilted her head back and kissed me on the neck.

"How'd it go at the doctor's yesterday?" I asked.

"Yeah, fine."

A familiar sound pierced the kitchen's calm; an ugly sound—metallic, throbbing, and urgent.

It was my nemesis, her iPhone.

"It's probably not work," she protested as she broke from me towards the window and her phone.

"It's always work," I said, but I'd made my peace with that.

She scooped up the phone, planted a rushed, wet kiss on my lips, and walked out to the hallway. "Don't let it burn."

I strained to listen to her call—still jealous, still insecure. I heard snatches of German, formal German; German meant work.

I took some chocolate from the fridge and went back to the window for more birdsong and sunshine, wondering what I had done to deserve a life so full of pleasure.

Nothing.

Absolutely nothing.

It was a loan whose terms I didn't know, whose contract I hadn't signed and could be recalled at any moment. Which was why it was so important to just enjoy it.

I was enjoying it very much.

She blew back into the room, her eyebrows low and knotted. "I have to do it."

"Turn off your phone? It is Saturday."

"PFFF." She returned to the stove, crackling away in her absence, wafts of burning onion and garlic filling the air. "You let it burn," she said, turning it down. "No. Quit, I mean. Of course. Too hot. *Grrr.*"

She was very stream of consciousness. You got used to it.

"Quit your job?" I asked. She'd been talking about quitting her job ever since I met her. It was just talk; she was that job—press for a major political party. It kept her very busy, but I liked that we never got enough of each other. That we weren't rushing through this dazzling beginning into some ordinary, dull rock of a middle.

"Do you think I should quit?" she asked, turning the hob down another notch.

"Er ... do *you* think you should?"

Her spatula work grew increasingly aggressive. "Why are you talking like a therapist?"

"What is it about your childhood that makes you think I'm talking like a therapist?"

3

She tipped chunks of pumpkin into the saucepan. "We used to stand for something, you know? I wouldn't even vote for them. And that's damning, right? I'm giving all my time to people I wouldn't even vote for. Who did you vote for in the past election?"

Evelyn was civic-minded, committed to improving the great human soup. She lived her values, had picked a political side and devoted her career—and a huge part of her free time—to help move the world in the direction she felt was right, while I was purely, selfishly Adam-minded, committed only to the relentless pursuit of my pleasure.

I let the question hang there so long she forgot about it.

"I'm going to do it," she said. "I should do it. I'm going to do it." She was firing the words towards the door, not me. This was a conversation with herself, in which I was merely a witness.

She wouldn't quit. If you do your job long enough, it becomes your identity, and identities are the hardest things to change. She picked up her phone, walked a lap of her kitchen island, then put it down again. "I will."

"I know," I said, but didn't mean.

"I will."

"Uh-huh."

"I will," she said louder.

"I know."

"After dinner," she clarified. "Yep."

This was the sort of *yep* younger maybes would bully in the playground. I went back to my task, the only one with which she trusted me: slicing things.

In this case, tomato.

There was a creak of the kitchen door and a small, lumpy shape appeared covered in thick black hair, scratching at the back of its head and yawning: Hemin, her room-mate.

"Are you slicing tomato or tickling?" he said, cackling as he moved across the kitchen to the open window. He was a short man with a cute little paunch. It was very possible to imagine him guarding a bridge and dispensing riddles. He was Kurdish, a communist, and about as new in Evelyn's life as I was. English was his fourth language, but he was improving rapidly.

"Look at this, Evelyn," he said, pointing to the juice dripping in a puddle on the tiled floor. "Look how he is cutting tomato."

I noticed a single gold strip hanging down from his left ear. He'd recently begun experimenting with piercings and facial hair, embracing the wider rules of acceptable masculinity offered here than Istanbul, where he'd lived for most of his life. Not all his experiments had been successes. Today, his gold earring and pencil moustache made him look like a cut-price Freddie Mercury impersonator.

I thrust the knife in his direction and flashed my teeth.

He cackled loudly. "With your technique, I have no fear. You are tickler, Adam."

"He's trying," Evelyn said, tipping a loose cloud of salt into the pan. "He's just not very competent yet."

"Trying to make mess, maybe? He cooks like capitalist, Evelyn. Capitalists don't need to know how to do anything because everyone does it for them," he clarified.

Hemin was unabashedly odd. A song you'd never heard, in a genre you couldn't place, but that grabbed your ear and didn't let go.

"Is that you volunteering to cut my tomatoes?" I noticed his nose had a cut across its bridge. "What happened to your nose?"

He felt along its bridge. "Is good nose. Strong nose."

"It's cut."

5

He poked it a little more, then shrugged. "I guess it was girl."

"Wild night, huh?" Evelyn asked. "Who is she? Was she? I mean, she obviously still exists, but you two, well. I'll stop." She turned back to the stove. Girls' shoes regularly appeared in the apartment hallway, but we saw few more than once.

Hemin grinned and seemed to have twice as many teeth as everyone else. "She is communist, like me."

"You want some stew, Hemin?" Evelyn asked.

"No, I am meeting someone." That grin widened. "Good communist girl."

"Ooh," said Evelyn. "Twice in one day?"

He looked up at the clock: 13:27.

"What time are you meeting?" I asked.

"One thirty."

"Shouldn't you be going then?"

He shrugged. "Time is capitalist concept."

"Take her some flowers," Evelyn said.

"I'm not taking her some flowers, Evelyn. My God. Communists don't need flowers," he said, moving back to the hallway. "We're happy with the dirt."

Evelyn reached into the packet of nuts lying on the kitchen island. Her hand returned empty.

"Did you eat all MY nuts?" she shouted after him.

"They are *our* nuts," he came back to protest.

"I bought them."

"The farmer." *Pause.* "Grew them."

"I compensated him."

"He was tricked, Evelyn," he said, making for the front door.

"So, you *did* eat them?"

"They have returned to the soil," he boomed as the door creaked open. "TO HORSE!" he said as if it were his destiny, fate, and burden instead of his local pub—a dark, smoky melting pot where lefty Turks and Kurds mingled in a broth of homemade communist zines, soapy beer, and ear-splitting 1970's psychedelia.

"Real character," I said as the front door slammed closed.

"Eh ..." she said, "he's just in a good mood because it's the weekend. You should see him on a Monday morning. He's like a wet fart. He calls in sick every other one. I don't know how he still has a job."

With the stew steaming in our bowls, we put on our coats and went through the living room and out onto the balcony, squeezing in next to each other in the nook she'd made from pallets and cushions.

"Delicious," I said as I finished the second mouthful. "Why are you not eating?"

She put down the bowl. "I'm doing it."

"Uh-huh." She wasn't going to do it.

"I am," she reassured herself as she stood up. "*Now.*"

She went back inside. I carried on devouring the stew. I ate so well now. Fish fingers and oven chips were a distant, calorific memory.

Ten minutes passed to the sound of heavy footsteps and low moaning. I put down the empty bowl, closed my eyes, and took a deep, satisfied breath.

I had her.

I had Berlin.

I had my apartment.

After nearly a decade in my previous relationship, it was wonderful to be back at the start; I wanted nothing to change. Nothing was going to change.

"You okay in there?" I shouted.

She came back to the door, still wearing her coat. "I

can't do it. I'll do it. Should I do it? UGH." She turned and strutted back inside before I could say anything.

I lifted myself up and peered in through the window. She was pacing around the room, phone to her ear.

Then there were words again. German words. Several minutes' worth of German words before she blustered into view, bending down to me and shouting, "I JUST QUIT MY JOB. I did. It's done. I quit."

She stood up.

Did I need to be happy for her? Was I happy for her? Was she happy for her? She leaned over the side of the balcony and screamed down into the street. "I JUST QUIT MY JOB. I HAVE NO JOB."

She turned in a circle, screaming some more, her breath short and rapid. "I DID IT. I DID IT. I AM THAT JOB. I WAS THAT JOB. I QUIT. GERMANS DON'T QUIT JOBS. Do I have any champagne? Yes! Exactly!" She ran off into the kitchen, returning with a bottle of champagne branded with the political event she'd stolen it from.

"I don't quit things. I stay in them too long; that's normally my thing," she said as she poured the first glass.

Was this good news? She worked insane hours for ungrateful people who continually undermined her. Now she was standing up for herself, making herself free for whatever would come next.

Yes, I decided. It was good news for her.

"Amazing," I said, and maybe even meant.

We toasted. "Who will I be if I'm not this?" she asked.

"Who were you before?"

"I don't even remember."

"Who do you want to be?"

Her nose twitched. "I don't really know."

She snuggled back in next to me and we sipped and listened to the sounds of sirens, the barking of car horns, and the rasping melody of a group of men singing drunkenly as they swayed across the pavement on a zigzag, circuitous path between bars.

"It's been a month," she said. "Since India."

We'd randomly met in a bar before she'd invited me to race a tuk-tuk across India with her just two days later, after her teammate dropped out at the last minute. A trip we began as strangers and returned as, well, whatever it was we were.

"That long?" I asked. "Feels shorter."

"Yep," she said. "I counted. I'm counting."

I had not been counting. She turned, so it was easier to make eye contact. "What do you ..." her eyebrows sank. She stopped to consider her wording. This was hard for her. "Are you happy with how it's going?"

"Deliriously," I said.

"What's next?" she asked.

"Why does something need to be next?"

"I'm free," she said as if it hadn't occurred to her until this very moment. She slid away a little and sat up straight. "I don't need to be in Berlin. I've not been able to say that for like a decade." She clasped my knee. "Let's run away. You and me. Me and you. Thelma and Louise-*Louis*."

I felt a tight tug in my chest. "But we just got started here?"

She put down her glass and raised her hands. "It's perfect. We can test this relationship in a new and exciting setting. I've never lived with a boyfriend," she said, her words rushing out now. "That would be interesting. Terrifying too. But I mean, you've done it before? *So. Yeah.* Great idea. Basically."

Tests sounded like work. *Why was she turning us into work?*

"I just bought a couch," I protested.

9

"It was €100, second-hand."

"I've barely been in Berlin the past few years."

"It's not going anywhere," she said as an ambulance raced past.

"Can't we just stay here? It'll be summer soon. We can spend it in the park, on a blanket."

"Istanbul?" she said with sudden urgency. "Yes! That's it. For a few months, at least."

I was getting whiplash. "Next year, maybe?"

Her mouth narrowed. "*No.* I did that job for eight years. What if I do the next another eight? It has to be now. With or without you."

The sirens were in my head this time. "You wouldn't?"

She laughed and chugged the rest of her champagne. "Wouldn't I?"

I remembered how wrong I'd been just a few minutes ago. "This is all happening very fast," I said.

"The good stuff always does."

"Are we the good stuff?"

She refilled our glasses. "There's one way to find out."

I thought back to the two weeks I'd spent in Istanbul during the Gezi Park demonstrations in 2013. A pivotal moment in my life that had given me a bug for weird destinations, sent me all the way around the world, twice, looking for its cure, resulted in this series of books, all my best stories, and I guess, ultimately—in a fluttering wing, butterfly-effect kind of way—to her and this moment.

"Why Istanbul?" I asked. "Because of Hemin?"

Hemin had lived there all his life, only moving to Berlin after a messy break-up, the imprisonment of his activist girlfriend, and because politically the writing on Turkey's wall was growing ever more slanderous of his people, the Kurds. Their oppression wasn't new, but the increased intensity of it was, as Turkish President Recep Tayyip Erdoğan's power has increased.

"There's just something about that city," she mused as if already there in her mind. "And it's politically interesting, cheap, beautiful, you like it, it's not that far away, I can improve my Turkish. See more of Kurdistan. And we'll spend a lot of time together, which means we can put this under some pressure, see what we've got here."

She was at it again. I didn't want tests or pressure. I didn't want to rush back to the middle. But I wanted her. And this was her—adventurous and spontaneous.

I scratched at various parts of my body, a common delaying technique. "I know nothing about the Kurds," I admitted. Before I'd met Hemin, I'd thought it was something that happened to milk. "But Turkey has an autocracy problem. And I've written some unflattering things about it."

"And I've been there on political delegations with politicians Erdoğan hates." She tucked in her lips. "I can imagine I'm on some kind of list. If we got in, we'd have to be careful not to feed the dictator, so to speak. And I don't know how fun it would be because everyone that can leave there has already fled."

"So, why are you suggesting it?"

"I'd like to see it again before Erdoğan destroys it completely."

"Why the rush? When did you get so decisive?"

"I'm playing the cards I've been dealt." She nodded sharply.

What I didn't know then, the reason for all this rushing, was that she had a secret. A big one. Something that would change everything about us.

"It doesn't seem like I have much choice here?" I said.

"Of course you do. I don't believe in ultimatums."

It went silent. She looked away.

"And yet ..." I said.

"And yet," she whispered.

"Can I think about it?"

She stuck out her tongue. "I'll give you fifteen minutes, okay?"

Reality was forking. On one future prong would be her and more of this. On the other ... not her and none of this. *What was there to think about?*

"I need a night," I lied, so she wouldn't feel as powerful as she really was. It was a yes. It had to be a yes.

"Fine," she said. "*Wimp.*"

"I'm worried that there might be some differing expect —" I said as my phone rang, which was uncommon. I wrestled it out of my pocket. It was my mother. I got up. "I said I'd do a call with my parents."

"Say hi from me."

I laughed. "They don't know you exist."

2

The plane hummed and whirred, gurgling a song of rapid acceleration as we hurtled through wispy clouds in a highly engineered aluminium baguette.

We had done it; she'd made us do it.

We were here, going there.

Inside, I was cartwheeling. Yes, I had been on many planes before; hundreds probably, but this was only the third one with her, and so it may as well have been my first.

Magic needs an audience. Together, she and I, were an audience—for each other, but also for the world, made anew by our shared, excited, sentimental gaze.

She turned from looking at the window to me. We swapped wide grins.

"Did you ever hear the one about how Fidel Castro killed JFK?" she said, a mad glint in her ocean-blue eyes, a thin line of intrigue curling her upper lip. "Pretty wild, I'll agree. But I don't know ... the world is pretty wild, right? And Fidel was badass. Some of them hats? Epic hats."

"Don't forget the beards."

She smiled that wide, toothy smile, just a little of her tongue poking out. "Grow a Fidel beard. It'll be hot."

I stroked at my patchy, pitiful, puny stubble. "My hair is just too thin. I think, well, I'm just not very dictatorial?"

Two enormous eyes popped over the seat in front of Evelyn's. It was the toddler she'd cooed over during boarding. Thick, curly black hair and owl's eyes. It had been asleep until now, and standing on its mother's lap, remarked us with bemused acceptance. I guess you're bemused a lot when you're eighteen months old; you learn to roll with it.

Evelyn blew it a raspberry; it laughed.

She went cross-eyed; it laughed some more.

I danced and clicked my fingers; it looked confused until Evelyn joined in. "Shake it shake it shake it shake it," she sang and now the child recognised human dancing and bobbed its head. "Shake it, shake it."

It was a really tender moment; one of many lately.

"She's gorgeous," Evelyn said as its mother shoved a dummy into its mouth. Its head dropped back down from view. I pulled my Kindle up from the seat pocket. "Do you mind if I read? I have to know how this book ends."

"Is it about Turkey?"

"No."

"Oh," she said with surprise. "I usually read about the place I'm going to. I thought everyone did that. Do you do research for your travel books?"

"Not really, no. But I'm done with books, anyway. Memoir is ..." I winced. I'd been unable to write a word since we'd met. "Happiness has nothing to say, I think."

"I have a lot to say," she quipped. "We could talk? Make some plans?"

"We can talk after. And no plans."

"Fine," she said, in a fake grump. "I'll suppose I'll read *my* book too then."

"Is it about Turkey?"

"*Passionate Marriage*," she said seriously. "It's this book from like the 90s, I think? It's about how you keep passion in a long marriage."

I cleared my throat. "Unless I'm gravely mistaken, you're not actually married? Passionately or otherwise? And your longest relationship is, what, like a year?"

Her forehead crinkled as she ran the numbers. "No, not even. So, you see why I need it, don't you?"

"It just seems a bit," I searched for a delicate word, "premature?"

"I've never lived with a boyfriend before. I'm nervous."

"It's just three months. A holiday, really."

"But it could become more, couldn't it?"

"Considering you're absolutely perfect in every way," I said, steering us away from that question, "why do you think your previous relationships failed so quickly and spectacularly?"

"Hmm." Her eyes rolled upwards. "I'd love to know that myself. Don't you think I'd love to know that? I'd ask them, but we're not on speaking terms."

"Not with any of them?"

"Oh God, no."

"I still talk to Annett."

"She said. *I mean*, you said. It is weird, though. I think I'm normal, and that I'm ..." Her head tilted. "Nice? Maybe too nice? Too accommodating?"

"You basically bullied me into this trip, so no."

She got up, unbuckled her seatbelt, stood up on her seat and clambered over me and into the aisle.

"I could have just moved?" I said as she landed ungracefully.

"Where would be the fun in that?"

She scampered down the aisle towards the toilets. I looked over at the man in the window seat. He'd been asleep since before take-off. The drinks cart rattled towards me. I knew that if this were a scene in a movie, I'd order champagne and then we'd get very tipsy, then go fool around in the bathroom.

But I hated champagne and drinking on planes.

"Do you have champagne?" I asked the male flight attendant as the cart reached our aisle because I knew she liked champagne, and that she was obviously the sort of person who drank on planes, and I wanted to make her happy.

The man smiled, and at its edges were conspiracy. "Celebrating?"

He handed me a mini-bottle and two plastic glasses. Plenty at this altitude.

"Well, well, well," she said when she returned, hands on her hips. I handed her the bottle and glasses, flipped up the table, and slid across to the middle seat so she could sit down.

"To the future," she said as our plastic flutes clinked.

"To the present," I corrected. The future was the future's problem.

The alcohol ran riot through our bloodstreams. Evelyn burst bright red, as usual, her skin blotching. She was like an octopus; everything she did and felt and ate and drank wrote messages all over her skin. The sentiment was clear this time: indulgence.

A few minutes later, it was my turn to excuse myself. On the way back from the toilet, the plane picked a pocket of turbulence and I sashayed down the aisle, already a little woozy.

"Surprise," she said, holding up a fresh bottle.

I did my best present voice. "Oh ... *great.*"

"To Turkey," she said as we cheers-ed.

"And Kurdistan," I added, because it interested me more.

I got hiccups. Evelyn went the colour of an over-ripe tomato. Eyelids grew ruinously heavy. The man next to us was still asleep. She shook the empty bottle. "Another?"

I didn't want to spoil her fun. "I mean, if *you* want to?"

"Do you usually drink on planes?" she asked.

"Aren't you the sort of person who drinks on planes?" I said, not answering it.

She laughed. "No."

"Seriously?" I tutted. "Then why are we ... I hate drinking on planes!"

She scratched at her now very rosy cheek. "And do you even like champagne?"

"Um ..." I said.

"You don't, do you?" she guessed.

"No, but you do."

"No, I don't," she said.

"But you're always drinking it?"

"Yeah, because I steal it from events and it has alcohol in it. I go to a lot of events."

"Why did you order the second bottle then?" I asked.

"To make you happy."

"I only drank it to make you happy. We lie to each other," I said, slapping the back of my hand against my forehead dramatically. "It's all been a lie."

"Has it?" Her eyes bulged. "Do we?"

I raced back through the heady first month of our relationship, trying to spot other things we'd pretended to enjoy but were secretly gritting our teeth through.

"The classical concert?" I said, bouncing in my seat, certain we'd agree. It had been a surprise for her, but when booking it, I assumed all classical concerts were largely the same and played Beethoven's Fifth or that dum dum, de de de, dum dum one that everyone likes and that might also be Beethoven's Fifth? It was in a church we had almost to ourselves. The musicians were two sad-looking old men. One played a cello and the other what Evelyn later told me was a cembalo—it sounded like a whale being clubbed to death in a cupboard full of broken glass.

They did not play the hits. I was the only dum dum.

"They were terrible," she said.

"You said you liked it at the time?"

She shuddered at the memory. "I didn't want to disappoint you. I don't actually like classical music."

"Yeah you do," I spluttered. "You own a piano."

"It's my childhood piano. I play it like once a year?" She raised her arms and wiggled her hips, as much as her narrow seat allowed. "I like hip-hop and music you can get down to."

"I thought ... don't all upper-middle-class people like classical music?"

Her mouth narrowed. "I don't even know where to start with that sentence. And aren't you upper-middle class?"

"What? I'm a chav, basically. My family are cockney pickpockets. There's barely a full set of teeth between us."

"The drum course?" she asked suddenly. This one she'd booked.

"IT WAS A NIGHTMARE," I said, then lowered my voice in case I woke up the man. Rhythm was a place I'd heard good things about but always got lost on the way, too. She reached out to stroke my cheek. "And brave that you went back for day two. There was a wager that started at lunch about it actually. When you were in the toilet for ages."

"I was giving myself a motivation pep talk."

"You could have just told me and we could have left?"

"No, I couldn't of." I put my head in my hands. "This is wild." I took my hands away. "I read something interesting, but I'm not sure I can remember it because of all the champagne and everything's a bit spinny. There are wobbles, I guess, is what I'm saying?" I rubbed at my temples, summoning all my remaining powers of concentration. "In relationships, people aren't who they are, nor who the other person wants them to be, because they don't know what the other person wants us to be, so we're who we think the other person wants us to be." I firmed. "Who do you want me to be?"

"Just who you are," she said, taking her hand in mine. "We have to be honest. I need us to be honest, always. From now on. *Okay?*"

"Er ..." *Had I always been honest with her?* Didn't the classical concert and drum course show that we hadn't been? And I didn't know honesty was so important to her. I hadn't been thinking very long term about us. *Was I always honest with myself?*

"O-kay," I said reluctantly.

"Great," she said, but then averted her eyes, perhaps because she wasn't being honest with me; she still had that big secret.

"Wanna fool around in the bathroom?" I asked.

"Yuck."

3

Woozy, we disembarked from the plane and joined a queue, shuffling towards several tall, glass-enclosed immigration desks. Standing was difficult, on account of the fact that someone had tilted the ground. They'd also turned up all the lights, the bastards.

Behind the nearest immigration desk, a stern woman sat in a cloud of fluffy black hair. Immigration queues are terrifying places, even if you're asking for rights that, in theory, you have. And this time I was going to lie. Not to Evelyn—who apparently I was supposed to be brutally honest with from now on—but to this hirsute bureaucrat, or one of her colleagues.

I looked back down the queue for Evelyn. She was over by some tables, talking to someone, writing something down for them. A few minutes later, she reappeared, asking the person behind me if it was okay to join me in the queue.

"What were you doing?" I asked.

"Helping Nozomi."

"Who's Nozomi?"

"A Japanese lady. Spoke little English, and no Turkish. I

helped her with the form thingy." She nibbled her lip. "I also sort of said we'd share a taxi with her to the city."

"Are we taking a taxi? The bus will be way cheaper."

"Er ... well, yeah, it was hard to say no. *Sorry*. I know we should make decisions like that together. We're a team now."

"Are we? Well, that's not a big decision. You can decide things like that. It's fine."

She angled her head back towards Nozomi. "It's possible she didn't understand me, anyway."

"It's okay," I reassured. "It's nice to be nice. I like that you're nice."

"Oh, there's that kid," she said, and started frantically waving. "So cute."

We inched closer to the desks as Evelyn bounced on her feet and sang something under her breath. Previously, I would have assumed this was an upper-middle-class ballad, Enya perhaps. Now I wondered if it involved a Dr or a Dogg or maybe even a Pac or an Enemy, perhaps of the Public.

The line wasn't long, just two dozen foreigners deep. The one for Turkish nationals returning home was three times the length. Tourism had collapsed, and the economy was speeding into a recession.

"What exactly is going on in Turkey?" I asked.

"You don't follow the news?"

"No, but sometimes it follows me and ruins my day anyway."

She took a deep breath. "Well, it's complicated."

"Why don't you put that brilliant mind of yours to use in making it simple?"

She rubbed an eye, opened her mouth, closed her mouth, hiccuped, then began. "Think of it as a hundred-year-long ideological fight between two teams, basically. Team Devout and Team Secular."

I nodded. "Two teams, got it. Are they even?"

She shrugged. "Pretty much, yeah? Team Secular has the big cities, Team Devout the heartlands. What's special in Turkey is that Team Devout doesn't actually care much about democracy. In fact, a lot of them want to scrap it and put the Imams in charge. Atatürk." She stopped. "You know about Atatürk, right?"

"The guy that founded the country after the first world war."

"Very good. Well, he knew he couldn't let Team Devout's leaders get elected. That if he did, they'd try to overthrow democracy. So, he made the military like a ..." She stopped, blinked, considered her wording. "A highly armed referee? Basically. There to guard democracy."

"Did they ever need it?" I asked.

"Oh yeah. Many times. Turkey is all about the coup."

"Is Erdoğan on Team Devout?"

"You're jumping ahead. I'm jumping too." She rubbed her elbow. "It hurts me to summarise something so complicated like this, but your eyes are glazing over."

I burped into my fist. "Sorry. It's the booze. You're doing a great job."

"Last bit. Erdoğan was mayor of Istanbul for a while but got a bit Islamic, and the military threw him out. He went away for a while to lick his wounds. He came back with a new party called AKP that he promised wasn't Islamic. People remembered he did a good job with Istanbul, and so he got back in."

"Crazy."

"No, the crazy stuff happened after that. In 2008, he presented all these documents, probably most of which were fake. They showed a deep state conspiracy. It was called," her hands balled into fists, "what was the word ... Ergenekon, I think?" She frowned. "I might be pronouncing that wrong."

"Let me guess, the documents showed all his enemies from Team Secular were actually corrupt?"

"Bingo."

"They should have called it Erdogeddon."

She laughed. "A missed opportunity there for sure. They put like five hundred people in prison, and after that, he could do what he wanted. Now he's showing his very Islamic colours and now we are where we are. Aren't we?"

"What about the military?"

"He's done a good job of weakening them, too."

"Thank you. That was surprisingly informative."

We were near the front now. "What happens if we don't get in?" I asked. "Do you think they just send us home?"

"If we're lucky," she said. "Did you see what happened to those Red Cross workers last week? They're all in prison now. Red Cross workers are enemies of the state?" she scoffed. "This country's falling apart."

A woman in a niqab passed through the gate, followed by her husband. I pulled out my passport from my back pocket. "Have a look at this photo," I said joking, "I still had hair."

I handed it over. It was not my photo that she seemed interested in, then incensed by, as her face flushed red and her jaw clamped. "Why is your name different?"

"It's not different." I snatched it back from her and checked.

"You have two first names," she hissed.

"That's a middle name." Middle names are less common in Germany.

"Why did you never tell me you have a middle name?"

"Why would I tell you?"

"It's important."

"It's *Richard*. I haven't used it in a decade."

"You lied about it."

Was this some kind of game? I actually wished there was a referee listening who could back up that what she was saying with ridiculous. "Did you ever ask me if I had a middle name?"

"Yes," she said, but too quickly, then looked away and down. "Probably."

"I didn't lie about it. That's stupid."

All the blood rushed to her face. She flapped her hand, trying to fan herself, taking deep breaths.

"What's going on?" I asked. "You look like you're having a panic attack."

"I'm sorry," she said, wheezing. "I'm ... there's some ..." She blinked away a tear. "I think I have some issues."

"About lies? Not that this was a lie."

"About my partners not being who they said they were."

I knew her last two serious boyfriends had turned out to be very liberal with the truth, but I didn't know the scars of that might not have healed.

I handed her my water.

"Did I ever tell you the story about how James and I split?" she said after a few gulps.

"I don't think so, no."

She looked at the queue, perhaps deciding if she had time to tell it. "I don't usually tell people. It's a bit embarrassing, but, I think ... I actually met him via his room-mate, Rob. It was Rob I had the crush on, but it didn't go anywhere. And then I was with James. One day I was studying at home and Rob called me and said I had to come over immediately. He wouldn't say why. When I got there, the front door was ajar, so I walked in. I went towards

24

James's room, and it was very obvious from the noise that he was in there having sex with another woman." She took another long breath to steel herself. "Sorry, haven't told this story in a while."

"It's okay, you don't have to."

"I think maybe I do, though?"

"Take your time," I said, but all I thought was—what an incredible idiot. She was, frankly, just an embarrassment of genetic and intellectual riches. How could she not be enough?

"I was, well, I went numb. I just stood there in the hallway, listening. She was putting on a hell of a show. Fakest orgasm I ever heard."

"You sure it was James?"

"I knew his sex sounds, obviously. We hadn't been dating that long, and he was a shit boyfriend, but the betrayal really stung."

I rubbed her shoulder. "Of course it did. That's horrible. Did you confront him? Or them?"

"Oh God no. I mean, at that point it was done. I went to leave, but as I passed the kitchen, I saw his passport lying there on the table. He was supposed to go to Amsterdam that evening for a stag do. I was so angry I got the kitchen scissors from the drawer, and I was just about to cut it up when I flicked to the photo page. HE HAD A DIFFERENT NAME. He'd always told me he was called James."

"I left, told him I knew, and then blocked his number. He wrote me a long e-mail later and tried to explain and stuff. I found out later from Rob that he changed his name to James when he came to Germany. Something about wanting a fresh start. I'm not sure though, I think maybe there was something in his past he was hiding from."

I wrapped her in a tight hug. The honest pact made more sense now. "I'm sorry that happened to you."

She broke away. "I think seeing your passport triggered some things."

"I didn't lie," I said. "I did nothing wrong."

She hugged me this time. "I overreacted. I'm sorry."

We split to go to separate immigration desks. "Your job?" the public official asked as she scrutinised my arrival form.

"Programmer," I lied. She glanced up as if she'd be able to judge my profession from my face: a white man in his thirties, wearing glasses?

Tick.

"This address?" she pointed at the address of our apartment, her eyebrow raised. "Tarlabaşı?"

"Uh-huh," I said, feigning confidence. Hemin had picked the area. Oh ... wait ... *Hemin* had picked the area.

Too late now.

The stamp hovered over the page in my passport. I looked at Evelyn as the electronic gate beside her booth opened. She looked back, hesitated for a second, dropped her head, then walked through the barrier.

4

An hour later, we stepped out of the taxi and onto a steep street that plunged down into the throat of Tarlabaşı.

Evelyn had presented Hemin with a shortlist of twenty apartments, nineteen of which were rejected immediately. Tarlabaşı was the only one he would entertain. Reading the listing, he stroked his chin, blew on the lip of his beer bottle, and nodded. "Freaks, foreigners, and refugees," he said with begrudging respect. "They are destroying it brick by brick. But the people fight. In Tarlabaşı, they fight."

That was enough for us. All around the taxi, life was spilling from the narrow pavements onto the road. Anyone that could shout, was shouting—about the things they had for sale, for the things they wanted, at people to move, at other people to stay and come drink tea from a tiny glass cup as they stood chatting on steps in front of house doors, pretending not to watch the transvestite in a short leather skirt walk up the road.

Transvestites? In an increasingly Islamified Istanbul?

Standing at the boot of our canary-yellow taxi, we said goodbye to Nozomi and watched our driver have a spirited discussion with another of its brethren coming the opposing direction. Our taxi won, its humbled rival reversed, and our driver popped the boot to free our luggage.

I wrapped my arms around my suitcase and heaved.

It didn't move.

It would not be so easily and casually moved.

Before I met Evelyn, I travelled so lightly even the softest breeze of serendipity could blow me. New relationships are great catalysts for change; this one had made me stupendously vain. I had a partner who cared how she looked, and who fluttered through Berlin's urban jungle like an immaculately accessorised bird of paradise. So, I had to care too. In my monster suitcase was every item of clothing I owned, a few things I'd stolen from more fashionable friends, and twenty-four shirts.

Twenty-four.

Before I met her, I thought creases were a myth invented by the patriarchy to keep women in servitude. Now, I could be found a hot iron in my hand, chasing the imperfections from a stubborn collar.

I planted my feet, bent my knees, and yanked it free. Evelyn watched on, her modestly sized backpack over her shoulder, soaking in the hubbub of our busy street, staring lovelorn at the facade of our new (holiday) home.

Her eyes swept down the road and she laughed, pointing to the sign on the building next door: *HDP*. "We came here to not be political, and moved in next door to the HDP," she said.

"Who?"

"The HDP is the Kurdish party, basically."

"Are they allowed to exist?"

"Exist, yes," she said, opening the small black gate to our building. "Do anything meaningful with that existence? Nope."

A group of men had been sitting on the building's steps

playing backgammon. They leapt up, encircled my suitcase and, between them, made light work of getting it up the steps to our front door, which opened, as if by magic, to reveal a lady holding a vacuum cleaner.

"Andrea?" Evelyn asked.

"Cleaner," the woman replied, waving us in through a door of such incredible heft, it could have secured a bank vault in the Wild West.

It weighed half as much as my suitcase.

"Really kind," I said, thanking the men a triple-digit number of times while bowing. "This door, Evelyn. Have you seen how thick it is? Do they have a crime problem here?" I followed them both down the hallway to a steep, spiral staircase.

I looked down at my suitcase. "I'll do it in stages," I shouted up. "A clump at a time."

Evelyn met me at our open apartment door, which was just as thick as the one downstairs. "So, full disclosure, a little smaller than I hoped."

"Did you ask the owner how many square metres it was?"

"She said seventy-five, but I think she included the terrace. And the terrace is about thirty square metres."

The apartment was shaped like a slice of cheese. Its base was the wide terrace that led to the bedroom, which connected to a hallway kitchen that took you past the bathroom and into a narrow living room whose point was a window that overlooked the main street; a street full of unusually shaped buildings.

We'd be able to get away from each other, but it would take effort. I trailed Evelyn through the bedroom and out the open door to the apartment's crowning jewel—that enormous roof terrace.

"Just look at it," I said, giving a whistle of appreciation

at a view that snatched my breath, tucked it under its arm, and darted off down the hill with it.

"I'm scared," she said. "It's tiny. And there's no oven."

"We'll be out all the time anyway."

"Will we though, when we've this terrace, and this view?" She sighed. "Good thing we wanted a test."

"I didn't want a test." For a brief moment, I wondered if she'd deliberately booked something this small; I shook the idea away. Even if she had, it was too late now. "No tests," I said, slipping my arm around her shoulder. "Just pleasure."

Because of the angle of the surrounding streets, and the steep drop below, we had a view across many of Tarlabaşı's twisting streets. The one beneath our first-floor terrace was a quiet backstreet with little car traffic, where a dozen children were running up the hill carrying bits of wood, then trying to sled back down. Nearby, groups of women sat clustered on doorsteps watching an elderly woman and a half dozen other rambunctious children clean a giant rug with water from a small yellow bucket, jumping up and down and skating across its surface to rinse it. Further down the street were several large, open sacks stooped over by women in bright headscarves.

"I think I've figured it out," I said after a few minutes of rapturous observation. "The entire street is some sort of mussel emporium. They're sorting them or opening them or something down there. Once they're ready, that harness comes down from the roof, see its coming down now, hoists the bags up, and then they go in that drum washing machine."

"Ah, that's the noise," she said. "Let's take a closer look."

Down on the street, we squeezed past a lorry delivering fruits and vegetables to the shop next door. We turned right, then right again and were now behind our apartment, approaching mussel street. Its entrance had a large metal archway covered in flags. Between the buildings, looped across the street, were washing lines full of clothes drying in the humid, late-afternoon heat. The narrow, dilapidated two- and three-storey homes were all squashed up at weird angles, framed by ivy that snaked between them, wrapping around the power lines.

"I feel like I've gone back in time," Evelyn said as we walked, feeling conspicuous in our foreignness. We passed a woman boiling tea over a small open fire, as another squatted next to her, using the same heat to roast eggplants.

A little girl ran up to me in a spotted yellow dress, a button on each shoulder. She had rosy cheeks and neat, clipped-back brown hair, and she took my hand, which seemed strange since Evelyn was next to me and looks like a Shakespearian sonnet brought to life, while I look like someone who'd try to blow up the moon with a ray gun of my own creation.

The girl babbled away. "Turkish?" I asked Evelyn, who had taken several courses in the language over the years, with little success.

She squinted. "Kurdish, I think."

"That's a good look for you," Evelyn said, smiling down at me and the child as we walked along, hand in hand.

"I like the ones you can give back best," I said.

"How old was your sister when she got pregnant?"

I flinched. Talking about our families annoyed me, but I didn't know why. "Twenty-nine?" I guessed. "No, thirty? But everything happens earlier in the UK since we only study for like five minutes."

"Would you want them in Germany or the UK?" she asked.

"My sister?"

"Kids."

I rolled my eyes. "I'm not—I have so much time. This

street is so, so beautiful." The kid let go and skipped away. We took the next street left, which ended at a metal staircase. Tarlabaşı was built around the edge of a hill and so its streets were at wildly different heights. Near the bottom, two young men sat on the lower steps. As we descended to them, the nearest fell backwards, hitting his head, but not seeming to notice. Then I saw the needle hanging from his arm. His friend was comatose, resting his head against the railings.

We stepped over them.

At the next bend, a taxi drove past, being chased by a grey dog snapping at its fuel cap. The dog strutted back, as it had clearly won this battle. On the other side of the road, a man sat crying on a bench, rubbing furiously at his head.

Hemin was right; this place was alive—with Kurds, Iraqis, Syrians, Africans, and maybe even a few Turks. Alive with rebels and outcasts and undocumented migrants pushed into this ghetto, huddling together for protection, in a country that had decided that its future belonged to one man and one faith.

We'd see a lot of that man in the next weeks. But not today. Today I had shirts to unpack.

Back in the apartment, Evelyn stood frowning before the open wardrobe. "Five hangers. Okay, so this is definitely a holiday apartment. Well. We'll make the best of it."

I removed a first heap of clothes from my suitcase and piled them on the bed. I'd brought everything up the stairs in trips.

"Oh shit," she said, a sudden alarm ringing in her head.

"What?"

"I know what I forgot to ask you. It's the single most important relationship question."

"Whether I have a middle name?"

"Hey." She shook her fist. "Don't make fun of me."

"Fine. Religion then?" I guessed.

"No, stupid." She looked down at my clothes. "Are you a piler or a spreader, basically?"

"A what now?"

"A piler or spreader?"

"Er ..." I put my finger in my ear. "I don't know?"

"Everyone knows, stupid."

"Stop calling me stupid."

"Stop being stupid, stupid."

"Is this like a thing?" I asked.

"It's the great divide between all people."

"Er ..." I twisted that finger. "If we don't match, is that it?"

She nodded solemnly. "That's it, yeah."

"This should be a first date question. Perhaps the first, first date question?"

"We wasted all ours talking about dictators," she said.

"We didn't know it was a date."

"We knew," she said with a wink, and I noticed she was in the same striped jumper she was wearing when we met at the airport for our trip to India. "So?" she asked. "Piler or spreader?"

"I think I don't understand the question," I said, removing several tight balls of socks from my suitcase.

"It's simple." She picked up a pair of my socks and threw it at me. "When there are many things around, do you spread them for easy access, or pile them?"

"I ..." I said confidently, before tripping over my tongue —spread too widely, or piled too high in my mouth. I was struggling for words, not because I didn't know the answer; there was no answer. The question, as best I could see, was bullshit. But the question represented something magical: she wanted to know everything about me. She already knew quite a lot about me to have reached a non-question like this. Yet she was still here, her interest burning inside of her, warming me in its glow, and it was the greatest of gifts and what I was most afraid of losing.

"Do you need me to repeat the question?" she asked, when I'd not replied for too long because I had gone dizzy turning corners in my mind.

I smiled. "I pile."

"Shit," she said, turning away, then back. "But it's so impractical."

"I just really, really love empty surfaces." I looked around for an empty surface to illustrate my point, but our stuff had already blanketed everything in this small room. "They're just so full of ... I don't know, potential?"

"So that's it," she said, taking her head in her hands. "It'll never work."

"But it's been working quite well?"

"Yeah, because we never had to live together and arrange the knick-knacks of our lives. I'm going to knock over all your stupid piles," she said, jumping forwards onto the bed, pushing over a neat pile of my shirts. I jumped on her and mock-bit her on the neck. We wrestled for a while, then I pried myself free, somehow, and continued unpacking my clothes while she, already unpacked, lay on the bed, cuddling her phone.

Time passed.

Day became night became day.

The young grew old.

The old expired.

The sun exploded.

The universe ended.

"Are you still hanging shirts?" she asked.

"Maybe."

"How many did you bring?"

"*Erm.* Well." My voice rose. "A few?"

She looked up at the overloaded hanger as I piled shirt fifteen on top of shirt fourteen. "It's an impressive pile, though."

"I know, right? I've experience."

We shared a goofy smile. There is nothing quite like a beginning—whether of a trip or a relationship. *How long could we stay in the beginning?*

5

In the late-afternoon light, we skipped down the stairs to go out for dinner. I wrapped my arm around Evelyn's shoulder and squeezed, feeling weightless as we strolled through the twisty alleys, marvelling at the cute red brick buildings of Galata, stopping to fuss cats. I'd forgotten how many there were and how much this city loved its *kedi*.

Wide, disgusting smiles on our faces, we giggled like schoolchildren on a day trip, stopping outside tourist shops to try on attractive hats my ordinary face couldn't compliment, no matter how much I tried to squint, pout, and smoulder.

As the first pangs of hunger prodded us, we had descended enough to reach the city's pride and joy: the Bosphorus—a bubbling blue cauldron that split both the city and two continents: Europe and Asia.

We gaped at the dozens of ferries bobbing on its surface. People got to commute on these—standing on the open top deck, the wind rustling their hair, staring at the dozens of minarets spiking up at the low clouds—instead of cramming on the top deck of a bus staring at the bumper of another bus, or nestling into the armpit of shower-phobic accountants as they whizzed through the claustrophobic caverns of a stuffy subway?

It didn't seem fair. It didn't seem right. "Istanbul is the most beautiful city in the world," she said, and it was the truest thing I'd ever heard.

The scene was a watercolour; too picturesque to be real. It reminded me of someone. "It's perfect," I replied as we kissed. "You're perfect."

We stayed in this magical place of perfection for about eight seconds. Two men broke it, passing us with square wooden boxes of shoe-cleaning equipment hoisted high on their shoulders. The second man dropped a brush, which clattered onto the floor next to my foot as a tram rattled alongside. He didn't hear me shout, so I bent down, picked the brush up and gave chase, waving it above my head.

He stopped, turned, raised his hand, a relieved smile spreading across his face as he skipped back towards me, his arm out. "Thank you, my friend," he said, taking the brush, then clasping my hand and wrist affectionately.

A warmth spread across me—the prickly heat of a good deed done.

What happened next happened quickly ... before I knew it, the roof of his wooden kit had flown open, and this humble shoeshiner was down and working at my calloused feet, brushes and polishes out, scrubbing my shoes free of their impurities.

I had helped him, and now he was helping me.

Only there was no debt.

And I wasn't wearing shoes.

I lifted my flip-flopped foot to display just how flagrantly redundant his task was, but he merely gripped its bottom and pulled it down, squeezed out his sponge, rubbing soapy water along the tiny strap between my toes.

This wasn't about whether I needed his services. No, it

was about something nobler. Something older. It was about honour, I suppose. About karma. About the sacred brother-hood binding all men.

"Tourist?" he asked as he ran a soggy brush along the flip-flop's outer edge. "Where from? How you like Istanbul?"

"Germany," I replied, picking one of his questions at random.

"Germany?" He stuck out his tongue. "Guten tag!" He turned to Evelyn. "Wife? Very beautiful."

"She's my *girlfriend*," I said, falling over the word. It was so ordinary, that word; so pedestrian. It wasn't a word I used for her.

"Girlfriend." He winked. "Kids? I have three kids. Hungry kids." He rubbed his belly. "Economy so bad now," he whined. "So, so bad. No tourists."

I nodded along, but this was all superfluous information in our I-helped-him-he-helped-me-karmic-rebalancing. He brushed the long outer edge of my other flip-flop before patting both feet in an *all-better-now* gesture.

I gave a slight bow, said thanks, and walked away.

"Thirty lira," he barked.

I froze, as did time, and the earth itself. Thirty lire was about €7. That would buy us a good dinner, or even two bad dinners. I turned back to find his face no long warm and inviting, but stern and pouting.

A crack had split the sacred brotherhood.

"Thirty lira," he repeated, his voice steel.

"I didn't even want my shoes cleaned." I lifted a foot. "And I'm not even wearing shoes!"

"Yes." He jutted out his chin. "And I clean them good."

"They're flip-flops."

"Thirty lira!" He poked me in the chest. I looked at Evelyn for help, but she was studying the floor. She hated awkwardness and was wracked with upper-middle-class guilt. She'd have paid; happily, even.

I took two steps towards her and away from him.

"Thirty lira," he repeated, following me. I stopped, pulled five lire (about €1) from my wallet, threw it at him and strode valiantly off onto Galata Bridge.

"Thirty!" he shouted, giving chase. "Come back. Thirty lira."

A tram whizzed by, and two ferries disappeared beneath the bridge. I was almost running now.

"THIRTY LIRA."

"THIRTY LIRA."

We reached a staircase and, trying to shake this shoe-shyster off, descended to where Evelyn said there were restaurants.

His shouts faded out. I checked and could no longer see him. I slowed down, relieved, pulling Evelyn back, smiling weakly at her, trying not to show my embarrassment.

"So awkward," she said, and we laughed nervously, trying to shrug off the interaction and get back to our earlier decadent, perfect, carefree headspace.

She might have managed it, but I did not.

Somewhere around the fifth restaurant we passed, she stopped and exchanged pleasantries with a woman holding a laminated menu. Then she pointed at something scaly in a blue bucket. Something that still had its eyes. Catch of the day, they were calling it.

The only fish I ate came wrapped in breadcrumbs or fell heaped from a can. Never were there eyes. She didn't even ask the price before ordering it.

Who was this woman?

This high roller?

This millionairess?

They showed us to stools, and she ordered a round of

Raki, the aniseed liquor that tastes like angry, rancid tooth-paste and had been the official national drink until newly pious Erdoğan changed it to Ayran, a non-alcoholic yoghurt drink that tasted better but gave none of Raki's relaxing buzz.

I wanted the buzz.

"Can we afford this?" I asked, still bruised from having spent five lire on a flip-flop wash.

Her brow furrowed. "I don't have a job." It was like it was news. "I've never not had a job. Do you pay close attention to money? Do I have to now?" Her shoulders slumped. "I suppose I do, don't I?"

The vinyl of the stool squeaked beneath my buttocks as I fidgeted, sitting up straighter to adopt a teacherly posture. "You get used to it."

"I always liked that about having a job," she continued. "You have little time, sure, or almost no time, in my case. But with what little you have, you get to let loose, you know?"

I gazed wistfully out at the middle-distance. "Wait until you find yourself lying in the park midday on a Tuesday, a bottle of Riesling beside you, your nose in a good book while the world toils around you. That feeling, that's ..." I lifted my chin, "priceless."

"Easy there, Mr Mastercard. And do you even drink wine? If I'm not pouring it? You have the taste buds of a four-year-old at a birthday party. I'm not even sure you can tell the difference between wine and champagne, can you?"

"Fizzier," I said, as if that one word settled a decade-long, multidisciplinary search for beverage clarity. "The Riesling was a literary flourish," I admitted. "I only started drinking wine when I met you. I drink water. From a tap. But don't ruin the fantasy."

I thought back over the day and where I'd spent money,

as I did every evening. I no longer recorded every expense as I had in the first tumultuous years of self-employment, terrified of being dragged back to the nine-to-five world of unsympathetic bosses in crappy companies underpaying me to market their app which—I don't know—promised to revolutionise how people shared their ... horse? While secretly only existing to circumvent horse laws and government horse taxes in the ruthless asset-stripping pursuit of undeserved horse profit.

"It was a good trick, right?" she said, gesturing back whence we had come: the narrow, cobbled lanes of Galata. She mimed a brush brushing, then tipped her head back and gave a wide-mouthed, somewhat horsey laugh.

"What trick?" I asked. I had not been tricked, merely shaken down by a representative of the Istanbul shoe mafia.

"Dropping the brush on purpose," she said.

I went both silent and cross-eyed. Space and time melted like a microwaved simile. I raised my small, thimble glass and sipped at the last disgusting dregs of my Raki. "He dropped the brush on purpose?" I said after an inordinate amount of miserable time spent berating myself for my stupidity.

"Of course," she confirmed.

"Why did you have to tell me?"

"It's the truth. Plus," her tone became slow and mocking, "I thought it was like AMAZINGLY obvious?" She laughed, tearing a chunk from the terrible, dry, crusty white bread in the little basket given free to every table, I think, to lower expectations for the actual meal.

She opened her mocking mouth and threw a chunk of this terrible bread into it, as she laughed loudly at my ignorance or, more likely, ignorances. Then she coughed, because this pseudo bread wasn't like normal, edible, yeasty bread. It would not be saliva-ed squidgy. Instead, it blocked her throat like a fat pebble, and soon she couldn't breathe and was choking and chugging water trying to dislodge it.

It was my turn to laugh.

This incensed her further as she gasped for air, her face and chest bright red and splotchy, her eyes swirling in panic.

It was almost enough to make me believe in karma, until she coughed hard, then opened her hand to reveal a shard of this completely undigested charlatan bread.

She grinned because she knew she had won.

I pushed my glasses higher up my nose. "I am mark, a schmuck, a rube."

"You didn't think how he dropped the brush was a bit too theatrical?" she asked.

"It is not my place to judge another man's theatre."

She squinted. "Does that sentence make sense?"

"I mean, just the chutzpah of it," I said, under my breath.

"It's actually pronounced *hutz-pah*," she corrected. "The c is silent."

I lead out a loud moan and crumpled forwards, rubbing the dome of my head in despair.

The bill arrived; our dinner had cost a whopping €25. Talking of chutzpah, they also charged us for that bread.

"They got us too!" I said, thrusting the bill at her.

"No," she replied, with a nonchalant kink of her neck. "That's what fresh fish costs somewhere with this view."

Had there been a view? I hadn't noticed, what with my being so blinded by anger. I was rarely tricked while travelling because I'm thrifty, cynical, and ethnically ambiguous. She had made me lower my guard and look at the result. An hour earlier, I had declared her perfect. But what kind of person got so much enjoyment from the misery of their partner? Her in my being tricked. Me in her choking while laughing at my being tricked.

Not perfect people, I decided.

And if we'd been wrong about each other already, on day one, how many more times would it happen?

A lot, actually. Starting the very next morning ...

6

"Argh," I moaned like a sad, uninspired pirate as I pulled the pillow over my head to block out the tinny call to prayer reverberating around the hills of Tarlabaşı, and beyond.

It was stupid o'clock in the morning.

The warbling bounced from mosque to mosque, each one amplifying and distorting, adding a brick to the garbled wall of sound crashing through the balcony doors, onto our formerly sleeping heads.

Everyone seemed keen we get up and acknowledge their God. I opened one eye. Evelyn was sitting up, her back to the metal bars of the headrest. "It's magical," she said, looking out through the open doors, tears forming at the edges of her eyes.

I rolled over, disgusted. "Too early for magic."

Outside, a dog barked.

A different dog barked in response.

A third dog threw its loud opinion in.

A cat joined the conversation.

This incensed ALL the world's dogs who answered en masse. I wrapped the pillow tighter to my head as a vehicle beeped, children squealed, a lorry reversed, and a baby burst into tears.

It was futile—the Tarlabaşı circus had thrown open the doors to the big top. I got out of bed, yawned, scratched my stomach, stretched my arms, and sloped out to the terrace where Evelyn was now sitting, knees pulled up to her chest, gazing out.

"My God would like lie-ins," I said, helping myself to the rest of her glass of water.

Her nose twitched. "Sacrifice is the point, no?"

"My God would hate those."

"What *would* your God want?"

"Ice cream. *Yours?*"

"Hmm," she pondered, tapping her chin. "People to spontaneously burst into song, like in musicals."

She got up and walked into the appliance-heavy hallway they were pretending was a kitchen. Soon, the smell of coffee filled the apartment and wafted out to the terrace. "What shall we do today?" she said when she returned, cup in hand.

I pretended to ponder. "How about *absolutely nothing?*"

"Nothing?" she said, as if the word had spikes. "There's an event later about conflict that looks fun, sort of. In a weird way."

"Fine by me."

"That's only an hour filled, though?"

"We could go back to bed?" I offered, beneath an elevated eyebrow of innuendo.

"Later," she said, patting my arm.

I leaned back and sighed contently, enjoying the novelty of no one wanting anything from us. Of being some-where that had no chores, no obligations, no certainties, and no routines—all the good parts of running away, basically.

Evelyn reached down to the table and picked up her phone: her new, non-work phone with a new, non-work number.

It didn't ring.

It didn't vibrate.

It didn't want anything from her.

She was free. She frowned at it. She put it down. She picked it up. She blew a raspberry. She put it down. She turned it over. She drummed her fingers on the tabletop.

"You're not very good at doing nothing, are you?" I said.

"It's new to me, I guess?"

"Well, go easy on yourself. It's only the first morning."

"I can do many things," she said, snickering. "But I can't do that. And we're here for a reason, right?"

"We're here because you wanted us to be here."

She grumbled and got up in search of her laptop. She came back an hour later to find me exactly where she'd left me.

"What have you been doing all this time?" she asked.

I shrugged. "Thinking."

"You've been on your phone, haven't you?"

I looked around the table and chairs. "I don't know where it is."

"You just sat here?"

"Yep."

She tugged her earlobe. "Just looking?"

"Well, kind of. I was thinking."

"What about?"

"Things. All the things, I guess?" I smiled. "You, of course. Me. *Us.*" I pointed down to the street. "Them down there. Death. Taxes. Book ideas. Yoghurt. That story you told me about walking into James's apartment to hear him having sex with someone else. How traumatic that must have been. Mars ice creams. You, again. *Us*. How awesome we are. Oh, and then some more you."

She sat down, a cocky smile on her face. "I'm in there a lot."

"It's incredible. It's like that fungus that takes control of the ant. Do you know about that?"

"No, but I love that you do."

My face tensed in concentration as I tried to remember the details. "It makes it into a sort of ant zombie and forces it to climb really high in grass so that something can eat it? I can't remember what or why."

She laughed. "It's okay, I think I get the idea. I am the fungus?"

"Yes."

Her head turned. "Is this a compliment?"

I lifted my shoulders. "I'm pretty sure it must be?"

"Thanks," she said and kissed the top of my head. "So, I've found a refugee centre a few streets away. Seems like it's mostly for Syrians. I'm going to volunteer."

"That's a good idea."

"You want to join?"

"Erm ..." I bit my lip. "Nah, I think I'm good."

"You too busy?"

"Kinda?" I said. "Also, I sort of don't really have any skills."

"You could teach English?" she said, but then lost confidence. While her English was almost flawless, she often asked me questions about nuances of grammar, frustrated when I couldn't explain them. I could only tell her what was right or wrong, never why. She was the same in German, of course—your native language is a gift you don't remember receiving, and rarely appreciate.

"Maybe you could just help out?" she said. "I don't know, cooking, cleaning or something?"

I laughed.

"Oh yeah, right. You can't cook." Her head tilted. "Cleaning then?"

"Yeah," I said, in a way that obviously meant no.

"You too good for cleaning?"

"It just ..." I exhaled. "I don't know. I only like doing things that scale."

"What does that mean, exactly?"

"It's just, like, if I write an article or something, then thousands of people can read it, or tens of thousands, or millions, or just like four people, but it's all the same effort for me. Same with a book. Although I'm done with books."

"So, you *are* too good for cleaning, is what you're saying?"

"You're the one with a cleaner, not me," I said. "It's just if it's about cleaning, that's a cheap skill, right? No specialism. I'd just be like an anti-dirt robot, and they can hire a cleaner here for what? Probably €2 an hour. I'd rather just give them the €2."

"Ah, so you're going to donate?"

It was getting tight in the corner I'd backed myself into. I blew out my cheeks. "Hypothetically, I meant. I don't believe in volunteering."

She crossed her arms and sat back in her chair. "In the meantime, people will still need food, blankets, jobs, money, help with their English."

"The state should provide those things and we pay for it with our taxes," I said haughtily. "Then I don't need to feel guilty for not giving my free time for something I'm bad at and doesn't scale, to help people abandoned by the system we've elected to be responsible for them, funded with our taxes."

"They're refugees. No one feels responsible for them, that's the point."

"Me badly mopping their hallways will not do much about that."

"You not mopping their hallway is going to do even less." Our tones were sharpening with each volley. She looked over her shoulder, either checking if people were listening, or for an escape route.

"I'll volunteer alone," she said with a roll of her eyes. "I also found a Turkish class for us."

"What do you mean, for us?"

"You wanted to join too, no?"

"Did I say that?"

Her mind darted through the long, twisty corridors of the past. "Actually, no. I just assumed you wouldn't spend three months in a country without trying to learn a bit of the language?"

She didn't know me well at all.

"Do you know how hard it was for me to learn German?" I said.

"You haven't really learned German."

"My point exactly."

"Turkish is really fun, though. It's like a weird little Lego language. Everything is a suffix of a suffix."

"It won't love me back."

She sighed. "You could just try it?"

"What time does it start?"

"Nine a.m."

I looked up at the sky. "You hear that?"

She tilted her head. "No."

"That knocking sound?"

"No."

"It's the final nail going in the coffin."

"Not funny," she said, as an arm flapped from a top-floor window. It was bangled. There was a middle-aged woman at the end. "Oooooooooo-ooooh," she called out. "Morning, you two.

"Who's that?" I asked through gritted teeth, while smiling and waving.

"No idea," Evelyn whispered.

"It's Andrea," she shouted. "I'm going to come down and we can have a bit of a natter."

"Oh, okay," Evelyn stood up. "I'll put the kettle on."

She moved through to the hallway–kitchen and unlatched the various bolts of our enormous front door.

"HERE I AM," a voice bellowed a few minutes later. "That tea ready? Already hotter than an Arab's armpit, it is." She looked around as if seeing the apartment for the first time. "Blooming lovely in here, isn't it?"

She was a lithe woman, with grey-blue eyes that pierced and prodded. She had mud-brown, wavy hair and seemed to move at double speed.

We returned to the terrace. In a couple of hours, the sun would find it, blasting it with heat until the early evening.

We sat near the large golden Buddha that was the balcony's signature eyesore. "This view, aye? Blimey. You're blooming lucky to have it. And me, of course." She fanned herself with her hand and raised her chin. "I'm what they call a *Superhost*. Did you see that? Yes, you've heard of superheroes. Well, I'm that for apartments. I've lovely reviews, did you read them? It's a cracking area once you get used to the gypsies and criminals and alcoholics. Everyone looks after everyone else, all of us down and out together."

Words rushed from her mouth, the brash, confident utterances of someone certain of their right to speak, convinced she was only saying what everyone was thinking. "Always keep the door closed and locked. A lot of unsavoury types around. You know, refugees and whatnot."

"The door is huge," I said.

She picked up the cup and sipped loudly from it, her lips smacking together. "Yessss."

"Any reason?" I prodded.

"Crime. Are you here for work?"

"Work? No," Evelyn said. "We're having a bit of a break. We're ... unemployed."

"Funemployed," I corrected.

"Blimey," said Andrea. "Why now? I mean. You're a bit late, aren't you? The city's not what it was. The only tourists we get these days are the bloody Arabs." The word was a sharp stone in her shoe. "Mucky, the Arabs. You should see the state of the apartments when they leave. And how they treat their women? Little better than they treat their dogs. Especially those from the Gulf states, and that's pretty much the only ones we get here now, to be honest. Since Erdoğan closed all the fun stuff, anyway."

She might be too honest, I decided, as Evelyn wriggled in her seat.

"Yeah," Andrea continued. "They come here to get plastic surgery. Hair implants. Nose jobs. You'll see them walking around all bandaged up like mummies." She pointed at the leftover fruit in the bowl on the table. "You done with that?" She grabbed a handful of grapes before we could answer. "Haven't had a bloody minute to myself. There's always something that needs doing. Such is the life of a Superhost."

"How long have you owned the building?" Evelyn asked.

"About seven years. I was coming out to my sixtieth birthday. I know I don't look it." She fluffed the back of her hair. "I realised I had nothing you might call a pension, so I bought it. It was quite cheap, seventy thousand pounds or so? Now the lira's down the toilet, so the money's useless anywhere but here. Bookings are down a third, and that's with prices half last year. It's not only the lira that's in the toilet, it's the whole bloody place. So sodding Islamic now. I mean, it always claimed to be, there's a mosque every other building blaring out that bloody racket five times a day, but back then, being Islamic meant only having one mistress." She laughed uproariously, entirely from her nose. "It was relaxed, you know? They're so bloody pious these days. Or pretending to be. I guess you need an enemy if you want to take power. Erdoğan picked fun, which is an odd enemy, isn't it?"

She reminded me of Hemin. It wasn't that she was nice, just that she had that curious, undefinable thing called charisma. Those that have it get away with a lot; perhaps too much.

She wasn't done yet. "Maybe it'll get better. You never know with the Turks. They're lazy buggers. I can say that because I married one."

She would have said it anyway.

"All they want to do is sit around and gossip over bloody backgammon. It's the women that work in this country. Did you meet the cleaner?"

"Yes, she's very nice," Evelyn said.

"Doesn't speak a sodding word of English."

"How's your Turkish?" I asked.

"Minimal. Anyway, lovely lady. Bloody useless cleaner, though." She rolled her eyes. "Pretty much ornamental, really. Past it, you know?" She rolled them again. "I keep her around because her husband just died. Useless, bloody, sodding alcoholic that he was. Got drunk and fell down the stairs, hit his head. Always said the bottle would kill him. I guess it did, in a funny way?" She snorted. "Better off without him, she is. Don't tell her I said that. Not that she'd understand anyway, bless her cotton socks."

Evelyn checked over her shoulder again. Many windows overlooked us, but I doubted behind them were people spoke English well to understand what Andrea was saying, or more accurately, slandering.

"Anything you need for the apartment?" she asked. "I doubt it, but fire away, while your Superhost is here."

We needed another thirty square metres and an oven, but that was a lot to ask her, Superhost or not.

"Yeah," I said, "now that you mention it. Do you have any more hangers?"

The sun continued its confident march across the terrace, and we retreated nearer and nearer to the apartment, sliding our chairs and table until there was nowhere to hide.

"I guess I best get back to work," Andrea said, standing up. "I'll pop in and see you again soon. Lovely to get to know you."

We'd said about ten words.

"She's a character," Evelyn whispered, as we were unsure where in the building she'd gone to. We were getting ready to go out. "How can you just casually admonish an entire culture? Or cultures. Do you think she was always like that, or did living here so long make her so? It is a pretty intense place."

"Sounds like one of those chicken–egg problems," I mused, stroking my chin.

Evelyn frowned. "We solved that decades ago."

"Did we? Where did the chicken come from then?"

"Whatever was before the chicken. I think they call it a proto-chicken?"

"So, the chicken came first?"

"No, the proto-chicken came first. That laid an egg, which another proto-chicken type thing fertilised, and their proto-chicken powers combined. Inside the egg was the first actual chicken." She bounced her thin eyebrows. "Neat, right?"

"So, the egg came first?"

"Yep."

"Crazy. Why didn't someone say we solved it? There should have been a big party or bank holiday or something."

"You're getting distracted," she said, lacing her shoes. "Google it later. It's called evolution. You'll like it."

I straightened my back. "I don't know much about proto-chickens, or even that there were proto-chickens, but I know a thing or two about Andrea's. People who move abroad, often because they don't fit in where they came from. That might be because their culture is weird, but it's more likely because they're weird. They find themselves somewhere they don't understand and that doesn't understand them, and that gives them a free pass because they're foreign. Suddenly there's all this extra space they fill with their burgeoning eccentricity. This sounding familiar?"

"You?" she said mockingly.

"Yeah."

"You are nothing like her. You're not odd. At least I hope you're not odd. I've not seen much oddness. You might be lazy and not very civic-minded, maybe? I'm not sure. That's new to me."

"Oh shit, we had our first fight," I said. "This was what I was afraid of. We never fought in Berlin."

"That wasn't a fight," she said dismissively. "Or was it?" She shook her head. "No. No one shouted. Or threw anything. Or slammed a door. Stormed off. Lied. It was a small conflict, maybe?" She looked at her phone. "Which is perfect, because the conflict resolution thing is about to start. Maybe we'll learn something useful?"

"More useful than proto-chickens and ant zombie fungus?"

She stuck out her tongue and opened the door.

7

"You look like a moderator, somehow," said Sam, a handsome young Iraqi in a grey baseball cap of a metal band, his forearm tattooed with black geometric shapes. He was the sort of person too cool to go to parties I wasn't cool enough to know I hadn't been invited to.

We were sitting on the rooftop of Pera Palace hotel—a famous city landmark, featured in the movies *Midnight Express* and *Skyfall*, and supposedly haunted. Mostly, it just seemed empty and sad; a lot of the city was like that now.

The event was called Chai Talks and funded by the EU. I was okay with conflict—it sure helped spice up the day—but here because I hoped we might make some friends.

They randomly assigned us to different tables. Along with Sam, there was a young Syrian woman in a headscarf who rarely met my eyes, and Abdullah, another Syrian— intense with a long, narrow face and a neat goatee. He was the oldest, perhaps in his late twenties.

Since the war in Syria, over three million refugees had come to Turkey, most settling in Istanbul with their lives made miserable by the fact the Turkish government won't give them official refugee status and with it, the right to work, which left them scrapping on the black market for accommodation and a livelihood.

A sheet of questions was on the table, designed to guide our conversations. "Okay then," I said, picking it up and reading the first question. "When you hear the word conflict, what do you think?"

They all scoffed. "Who wrote this?" Abdullah asked, spitting his words out like they were poisonous.

"Right," I said, reading down the sheet. "I'll skip to the next question. Question two: can you talk about a conflict from your life?"

"I can tell you about conflict," Abdullah snapped. "I can talk for hours about conflict. My life is conflict. Always conflict."

I put down the sheet. "When did you get to Istanbul?" I asked.

"One year ago. *Shit*. The time goes slow. Before I was in Syria, and you know what that's like. Every day, bombs and rockets." His English was confident but clipped, his words coming out bent but intact, like dropped tins. "You go crazy in that kind of environment." He looked at the other two. Sam had gazed off in the distance, stroking his forearm. The girl nodded, almost imperceptibly, as Abdullah kept talking, firing out his words as if this was his last chance. "Not knowing when it will start, when will it stop, who will be hit, running around try to find your family members. It is nightmare that never ends. You cannot wake."

His glare softened. "It's crazy, but there was a certain peace to that time. You have singular focus: keep family alive. You don't even care about yourself. Just family. Just younger brothers. Bombs exploding. I found them one time, together with my grandmother, hiding under the stairs. Sitting in line, arms and legs crossed."

I waited for the others to chime in, but they stayed silent. "When did you finally decide to leave?" I asked.

He looked away, frowning. "We stayed too long. They arrested my brother while walking through some checkpoint because he had same name as someone on warrant list." His eyes flared with anger. "Someone twenty years older than him and from a different province. He spent the next fifteen days in prison being tortured before finally being released without charge. Then I knew we had to get out. There is no society left when we can disappear at any moment, knowing that if the bombs don't get us, the government will."

Abdullah was talking 95 per cent of the time; I was failing as a moderator. "Sam, do you have a conflict?" I asked, trying to bring the other two in. Sam lit a cigarette, his hands trembling. "I guess my biggest is with my dad. It was similar to yours, Abdullah. It was about whether to leave or stay in Iraq once the war started. My dad said I had to stay and look after the family, that it was safe enough. But for me, there was nothing there." He swallowed. "No opportunities, no life."

"Are there opportunities here?" I asked.

He shrugged. "There's no war here, at least. If I could get work status, there'd be opportunities, sure. But I can't. It's also getting worse and worse politically." He tapped on the table. "Still, it's better than Iraq."

"I am sick of seeing his face," said Abdullah. Erdoğan was everywhere, looking sternly out from the top of lampposts or plastered across billboards, kissing babies and hugging grannies.

"People can't do their jobs anymore," Sam said. "My girlfriend is Spanish and a freelance journalist. At an event recently, someone from the Secret Service sidled up next to her. He didn't threaten her directly, but he told her all these details from her life. Made her aware just how much the state knows about her."

"Is she writing negative articles about Erdoğan?"

His lips pursed. "No, not really. But it doesn't even matter what you do, it's what you already did. Did you see the case of those cartoonists sentenced to prison for making fun of Erdoğan years ago? Or the ex-Miss Turkey?"

Evelyn had told me about them, yes. Erdoğan's skin thinned each year while his prison grew.

"What about you, Adam?" Sam asked. "What conflicts do you have?"

I laughed nervously. What could I answer? Did Evelyn and I fear the German government would wrongly arrest and torture us? Had we ever cowered from a bomb? Discovered our family members in a line under the stairs? Been forced to leave the country we were born in because there were no opportunities, to come to a country that didn't want us and wouldn't let us work, and then still have to conclude it was better than our home?

"No conflicts," I said. "Not right now, anyway. Nothing important."

It was very difficult to get the girl to talk. She spoke little English, and whenever Abdullah translated, he would quickly take over, switching the topic back to himself. He always referred to her as *Sister*. "Sister left after her brother and sister were killed. Sister travelled here with cousins. Sister likes it. Sister worries about future. Sister doesn't feel ready to get married. Sister like to get a job." He stopped interpreting. "Why do you want to get a job, Sister? Jobs are not for sisters."

"I'm sorry," I said.

"For what?" Sam asked.

I shrugged. "Everything?"

"It's not on you, dude."

The dude momentarily threw *me*, reminding me of a video I'd seen of a Metallica-listening party getting attacked somewhere in the Middle East, maybe even Iraq? Sam seemed like exactly the someone who would have been there, tapping his foot, banging his head, playing air-drums, dreaming of being born somewhere that tolerated subcultures and niches. A place that considers a fringe as something that accents the whole, rather than an aberration that threatens EVERYTHING.

"You said you're a writer? Write about us," said Abdullah. The other two murmured in agreement. "About what is happening to us. About how we are stuck here. About Syria. About conflict."

I flapped a hand. "It's just my mum buying my books. She hasn't let me in her garage in years."

"We need help," he said.

I nodded. "I know."

"You can help."

I wanted to believe him, but I didn't. "There are so many stories here," said Sam, lowering his eyes.

I remembered the conversation, or rather monologue, with Andrea. Were these the refugees she admonished? How many had she actually met? A refugee isn't an unsavoury type. And if they could choose, they'd choose to be anything else. A war has not happened to me. A war has happened to Abdullah, Sam, and Sister. From there, I don't consider doing the thing least likely to kill you as making a choice. It's simply your imperative. If you follow that imperative, you might end up in Benin, Berlin, or Istanbul. That's bad enough, but wherever you end up, you become saddled with this word people like Andrea can use to discredit you: *refugee*.

The event ended, and we walked the many various winding staircases back down to the lobby. Sam appeared with his girlfriend, a white tote bag strung over his bony shoulder. I sidled up to them. "Hey, man," I said, "what you up to now? Wanna go for a drink?"

"I'm going to a party with some friends," he said.

"Cool." I waited to be invited. It was like high school. No invite came. I considered inviting myself. I was ten years older than him. Why would he want to hang out with me?

"Have fun," I said, turning around and looking for Evelyn. She descended with her group, and I hugged her.

Abdullah appeared. "Ah, your wife? Very beautiful."

"What's happening now?" I asked.

"We're going for food," he said, and so we walked to a narrow fast-food restaurant, eating underwhelming falafel while Abdullah talked and talked, winding himself into a manic frenzy. "I will never find a wife here," he said as he tore at a piece of flatbread, shoving it deep into his mouth. "No way. No chance. There are no good Muslim women," he said, chewing loudly, "and I'm refugee."

"There's lots of refugees, though, no?" I said.

"Yes, but after time here all women get Westernised."

Evelyn stiffened. "What does that mean?"

"Western women make problems. Always problems."

"What do you want your wife to be like?" she asked.

"Women are to make the home." His eyes rolled round at the obviousness of this. "To raise children. Not for working," he said, scowling. "Not for being around men."

She finished chewing. "What if they want to work? To have a career?"

"This is not what *I* want."

"What about what *they* want?"

His head tipped back. "And I am old. So, so old. They say they want me, then reject me. Always the same, with these women."

"How old are you?" I asked.

"Thirty," he said, as if it were sixty. "Women today have too much power. They want to reject men."

"Maybe they just want to reject certain men?" Evelyn suggested delicately. She was so fair of face and light in tone, she could make almost everything sound like a compliment; a talent she seldom abused.

Abdullah leaned back in his metal chair and let out a huge, winding sigh. "We are stuck. Stuck in this life. It is shit, this life. I hate this life." His eyes stretched with anger and frustration. "But what I do? Where I go? Where I meet this woman? What I offer her? What she offer me? It is bad, this life. It is joke. It is no hope. It is nothing." He looked around the long table and into each pair of eyes, daring us to disagree.

No one did.

On the slow walk home, we detoured down İstiklal Avenue, the wide shopping thoroughfare that leads to Taksim Square—once the unofficial meeting place of the city's youth. Where they huddled on the raised concrete steps or lounged on the small patches of grass, playing music and cards over a beer. Talking, flirting, enjoying time away from the close, watchful eye of their families.

It was empty. The park remained and as concrete-heavy as ever. But no one was using it. The surrounding back-streets were just as desolate, with many stores, bars, and restaurants shuttered. "Was it always like this?" I asked, doubting my memories.

Evelyn had been here several times, and more recently than me. "No," she said.

"Andrea was right, there are no European tourists."

"Yeah," she agreed as we passed our twentieth bandaged man. "She was also right about the mummies." She stopped and turned, trying to get her bearings. "Didn't this street used to be full of bars? I'm sure I remember drinking in a lot of smoky bars around here."

"There's one, I think." I pointed. "Oh, no, that's just another shisha place. Is shisha actually part of Turkish culture?"

"No," she said. "It's Arabic."

We passed another boarded-up building and a restaurant so empty a man chased after us trying to convince us it had the best food in town.

"I'm sorry about earlier," she said.

I stopped mid-stride. "About what, specifically?"

"I don't know, all of it?"

I wondered if she was doing a technique she'd learned in *Passionate Marriage*. "It's very nice that you're willing to say sorry," I said. "But I think you're apologising that we couldn't agree, not because you think you did something wrong?"

She lowered her head. "Maybe."

"It's okay if we don't see the world the same. Better actually, there's more to explore."

"I think we do, though. Maybe that's what I'm apologising for?" She pointed back towards the event. "I was on the table next to yours. Our moderator was this Turkish guy who talked the whole time. A typical macho dude. I zoned out and listened to your table. It was so different. You made everyone feel really comfortable. You asked questions. You tried to make sure everyone talked equally. You make people feel good." She touched the top of her chest. "You make *me* feel good."

"That's ..." I blushed and looked at my shoes. "Nice." I didn't realise how much I wanted praise until I had it. It was like a second sun, just for me. She took my hand, and spying a small gap in the traffic, we skipped across the road.

"I think I'm just more motivated to help on a general

level, macro, while you're micro," she said as we rejoined the pavement on the other side.

"Maybe," I said, still not sure I was this praiseworthy.

"It's like ... with our apartments." She continued as we walked hand in hand. "Chris has your apartment now, right?"

"Yeah?" I said, not noticing an enormous hole in that pavement and tripping into her. "Ouch."

She kept me upright, wrapping her arm around my middle.

"Thanks," I said as I recovered my footing and shook out my ankle.

"I sublet mine, you know? I made an ad, deciding how much I thought the market would pay, and then upped it 10 per cent." I stopped. She raised her hands before I could interject. "That's not unethical, I know, but I bet you gave your apartment to Chris for as little money as you could?"

I laughed. "I'm not charging him anything."

Her eyes doubled in size. "What? You're paying for him to stay in your apartment?"

"He's not earning much at the moment. I wanted to help him."

"Exactly." She beamed. "See. Exactly what I mean. You draw the line differently. To your friends, you are fiercely loyal. Many of them mentioned have said that to me. No one would say that about me."

We broke apart to let people pass. "I haven't met many of your friends."

"Because I don't have many."

"But you're extremely wonderful, so I don't understand why that would be?"

"I'm a bit odd, I think? And scared of rejection. Often, it's easier to just hide in work. I remember my birthday, a few years ago. I really wanted to do something but was scared to impose on people, and it got nearer to the date, and I just couldn't do it. I had a different room-mate then, and she knew it was my birthday. I figured we'd drink a cocktail and eat a bit of cake. But she forgot, I guess? She didn't come home, and so I just sat there on my own, sad, eating an entire mini-cake and working."

I retook her hand. We waited to cross a road. "It was my fault." She shook her head. "But this isn't about me. I had a point. You don't look away, is what I'm trying to say. You ask questions. You're interested. And that makes people feel good. You are fundamentally good. That's why you can just sit there on a chair and think and stare, just being content with yourself. Your mind doesn't turn on you. Doesn't attack you. It has no reason to. That's rare. And you *do* contribute. Your books are a contribution. Are you really not going to write about this trip?"

"No."

She raised her chin. "That's a mistake."

"Now," I said as a small gap opened for us to rush across the road. "Abdullah and Sam said something similar," I continued as we entered our road. "I just feel like any moment I don't spend with you, just like drinking you in like the fine wine that you are, just enjoying us, is a wasted minute."

"You don't even like fine wine," she said, stopping me to hug. We were always hugging. Some days it felt like I was in a Japanese gameshow and we'd been superglued together. "I wish I saw me as you see me," she said.

"Me too."

A car started honking at us to move out of its way, the sixth to do this on our short walk. For a perfect city, this one had anger problems and really hated pedestrians.

"This trip isn't going to be what I expected, is it?" I said.

"What did you expect?"

"Pure unbridled hedonism, mostly?" I opened our gate. "But maybe that's not a very sustainable state? And the people we're meeting—Andrea, the people at Chai Talks, the mussel washers, shoe-cleaning shysters, heroin addicts with needles hanging from their arms—this city has changed. It's like it's in mourning."

I unlocked the door. "No," she said as she entered. "It's going to be more interesting and challenging. And I mean, Hemin warned us."

"Yes," I said, heaving it closed. "Why didn't we listen?"

8

After three weeks in Istanbul, life had taken on a familiar rhythm. The refugee centre was closed for the summer, so Evelyn busied herself with Turkish class. I'd pretend to be asleep until she left each morning, then I'd laze around on the terrace, researching areas and attractions before wandering out into my day.

I'd drop a pin for Evelyn, and we'd lunch extravagantly, talk, read, and gossip. No matter how often Istanbul tried to run us over, trip us up, send us on long detours while it built even more motorways, squeeze us between pollution-spewing buses and vendors with overflowing carts of scrap metal, we walked.

Anywhere we couldn't walk, we took the ferry.

We learned Istanbul was an easy city to look at but a hard city to be in a relationship with. Beneath its attractive veneer, it was a hot mess. An abusive partner who didn't need sleep, had very firm opinions about how we should behave, never gave us personal space, and was having a very public affair with the automobile.

Regardless, those three weeks were some of the most relaxing, enjoyable times of my life.

Little happened; that was by design.

Until ... in bed one morning—pretending to sleep but surreptitiously reading on my phone—as Evelyn busied herself for class. Hearing the front door thud closed, I got up to find chocolate. Sitting on the terrace, scrolling through the Internet's freshest memes, I became distracted by sounds of commotion from the front of the apartment—a commercial street always in a state of low-level chaos.

I got up from my chair, yawned, scratched my stomach, and strolled languidly inside, stopping in the kitchen to stuff half a banana into my mouth. Sustenance for the five-step journey to the living room.

Why was it so ... dark? I stopped abruptly, seeing the windows blocked by the top of an enormous armoured police juggernaut. I dropped to the floor, smushing the other half of the banana against my leg. My heart raced loudly enough that I could hear it in my ears, as I dropped my forehead to the wooden floor and let out an unbecoming whimper.

They couldn't be here for me, could they? Because of my books? Because of the things I'd written about Erdoğan?

I crawled forwards, pulling myself up with the window's ledge to peek out. Twenty police officers carrying riot shields swarmed from that vehicle, taking up crouched positions along the small wall that separated our building from the street. Another armoured police death star trundled down the hill, parking next to the first. The road blocked in both directions now.

I dropped back to the floor, turned, and scrambled towards the bedroom—wiping banana residue from my thigh on a discarded sock of Evelyn's—before throwing on yesterday's clothes. Out on the terrace, I looked for a way down, should I need to escape—*did I need to escape? Yes, needed to escape.*

There was no way down. The drop was too big. Figuring it was best to have someone know what was happening as early as possible, even though nothing was happening, right? I took out my phone.

Adam: Police. Lots of police here.
Evelyn: Where?
Adam: Outside the front door.
Evelyn: Shit.
Adam: I'm sort of maybe freaking out?
Evelyn: It's not irrational to fear the police in a police state. I'm coming back.
Adam: No, you don't need to come back. It's probably nothing.

Wanting to avoid any windows—in case I was casually or even formally sniper-ed—I paced the bedroom, scratching deep worry lines into my back. I had two of the thickest doors in home security history between me and them. *Not that they could be here for me, could they?*

That was crazy thinking. But then, all the stuff in the press? Evelyn and I discussed the new arrests each night over dinner. We didn't read about them in the Turkish media, of course, but the German—they still had the freedom to report the overreaches of a government that seemed to have an extraordinarily large number of enemies. What happened to Sam's journalist girlfriend was trivial compared to what they were doing now.

I had written some things, uncomplimentary things about Erdoğan, but that was years ago, and who had read them? Almost no one. And they weren't that mean. And I was a nobody.

Yet, on a quiet Wednesday morning, a massive show of force was taking place beneath my windows. I rubbed my head and paced back and forth in front of the terrace's statue of Buddha, whose sanguine expression mocked me as I gulped and hyperventilated before returning to the living room, crawling the last metre to the windows on my stomach.

Two smaller police vans arrived. Otherwise, the street was eerily quiet. In Berlin, people would gather to see what was going on, while perhaps sharing their opinion about whether it was fair and just. If it wasn't, there would be a demonstration. If the demonstration wasn't fair and just, a counterdemonstration. I'd never seen a counter-counter-demonstration, but I wouldn't rule it out. Berlin was that sort of place: participatory, vocal, inclusive, demanding of its rights.

It used to be like that here. I had taken part in those demonstrations even, in Taksim Square. Now, I noticed people didn't want to interact with the police anymore. They hurried along about their business, averting their eyes.

I went to the bedroom and lay down on the bed, panic rising from my stomach up into my oesophagus. I took long breaths in, held them, and slowly let them go. We lived in Tarlabaşı, a smuggler's den. They might be here for any of us, I reassured myself.

Every now and again you're given little tests of your character. Moments that reveal your constitution. This was one. I didn't need to play the what-would-you-have-done-in-Nazi-Germany game. I would have cowered, mostly, with a little kowtowing thrown in for good measure.

I sat up: this needed to be resolved, one way or another. I'd go outside and buy myself a Mars ice cream. That way

I'd find out if they were here for me, and if they weren't, I'd have a Mars ice cream.

I opened the apartment door, descended the stairs and, with trembling hands, opened the building's low gate, remembering I wasn't supposed to know the police were here. I was just an innocent, everyday person, after all. Not a memoirist who had written about the Gezi Park demonstrations in a book called *Don't Go There*.

The gate squeaked. I stepped through, turning my head comically slowly towards the—absurd number of crouching —police officers. I opened my mouth, forming my best, most surprised, open-mouthed O.

Police?! Here?! On my street?

I lifted my hand up to my chest in simulated shock. I waited. Nothing happened. They looked past me, towards our neighbour—the HDP building.

The HDP building, of course!

Occam's razor sliced at my panic, and while it didn't kill it, it left it wounded, apologetic, and embarrassed. I walked up the hill, being sure to amble as if I didn't have a care in the world—just a normal, spineless man not causing anyone problems, cowering, a little kowtowing perhaps, off to get his privileged-white-European-ass a breakfast Mars ice cream.

Sitting on a stoop, a few houses behind the police, eating my ice cream, I looked at the spectacle and chastised myself for being such a spectacular idiot. As I sat there, deep breathing away my fear and shame, I understood something: this is how everyone in a totalitarian state feels, all the time.

If you are cold, you can put on more layers until you become warm—you can give yourself comfort.

If you live under an increasingly tyrannical government, working without oversight, you're ... screwed. Once a state shows its wrath will be dispensed arbitrarily and incommensurately, no one knows if the knock on the door in the dead of the night, the unmarked van trundling to a stop in front of the house, the firm tap on the shoulder in the crowded street, or the call telling you to drop by your boss's office is the thing you have long dreaded. What will shatter your life into so many pieces you can't hope to make it whole.

There is no comfort you can give yourself. No way to feel safe.

You can accept what's happening to you and your culture, hoping your complicity hides you, but then you must also live with the shame of that capitulation. With knowing that you are doing nothing to help break the chains that bind you. Chains that will keep tightening.

This is fascism's achievement. Erdoğan's achievement: the degradation of *Normal*. I've travelled for a decade—often to places people are trying to get away from—to make palpable the immense fortune of my birth.

At this moment, I appreciated it enormously. This gnawing sense of deep, malevolent dread was nothing I wanted again. And it doesn't matter if you're being irrational, illogical, or paranoid, your feelings at any moment *are* your reality.

I felt stressed, mostly, and a bit sick, perhaps from my very unhealthy breakfast. It would be fine for me. The outcasts of Tarlabaşı, Abdullah, Sam, Sister, and the millions of other Syrian refugees, not to mention the Kurds and liberal, non-believing Turks, wouldn't be so lucky.

I took out my phone.

Adam: False alarm.

I put it back in my pocket just as a sweaty, out-of-breath blonde mass of tangled hair collapsed into me, knocking me onto my back with the full force of her urgent hug. "You're okay?" she said, wheezing.

"I'm okay."

Her eyes narrowed. "Are you eating a—never mind." She pulled back and fanned herself. "Oh, God. I ran all the way here. Got really panicked something was going to happen to you and," she clutched her stomach, "stitch. Ouch. Yeah." She shook her head. "That you were going to end up in a jail and I would never see you again or only in like years and it would be too late."

"I'm sorry," I said. "I overreacted." I pointed towards our apartment. "They're here for the HDP."

She looked in its direction. "Oh no."

She stood up and wiped the sweat from her forehead.

"It's nice that you ran," I said. "Wait, you wouldn't even wait years for me?"

I expected her to laugh, but her face cracked. "I can't," she said, her voice shaking. "There's something I need to tell you. Something I've not been honest about. Bad news."

9

I stood up. "We should get a nice cup of tea," I blurted out, gesturing to the tea shop opposite.

"You don't even like tea. You say it's just hot leaves," she said between rapid breaths. "Oh, God, I'm really unfit."

I flapped my hands, trying to release the tension of the last hour. "I think British people instinctively link a crisis and tea. Is this a crisis?" I glanced towards the police. "I just survived a crisis. I can't do another crisis."

"It's not a full crisis," she said as I reached for her hand under the guise of emotional support, but really just to check if she'd let me take it.

She let me. We passed the police slowly and went inside. Side by side on the bed, we lay looking up at the ceiling. I was happy to see it. That I'd get to keep seeing it and her. I wasn't worried about her news. How bad could it really be?

I rolled over towards her and rested my hand on her stomach.

"You're squeezing," she said.

"Yep."

"This is serious."

"No, out there is serious. I thought I was going to prison. This is squeezing."

She picked up my hand and moved it off her. She shuffled a few centimetres away, towards the terrace's open door, sat up, squished some pillow behind her, and drew her legs up to her chin, looking down at me. "This is serious," she said again.

"Oh," I said, because I was starting to believe her. I scooted down to the foot of the bed, my back to the bars, so we were opposite each other and could make meaningful eye contact.

We did not make meaningful eye contact.

She looked down at the floor on her right and in a low, sad voice said, "I went to the doctors after we got back from India." She blinked away a tear. "I did some tests. I didn't want to talk to you about them yet, because we weren't really at that stage, or anything, but, well ..." her voice broke, "I don't really know what stage we are at. I hate thinking in stages." She sobbed, looking around for a tissue. There were none, and she stumbled on. "But, well, it took my sister an age to conceive, and I'm thirty-four and so ..." She squeezed her eyes shut.

The colour drained from my vision.

We were those people—strangers who meet and fall into bed, mad with lust, staying there in a sticky frenzy until they accidentally make a human, prolonging a madness that would have, should have, ended a few months later in mutual, tender acceptance of their fundamental incompatibility.

"You're pregnant," I said, lightheaded. She let out an animal howl. "Hey, come here," I said, shocked at the depth of this emotion. I crawled towards her, pulling her leg, then body down, wrapping her in my arms as she sobbed and sobbed. "No," she said, wiping her nose with the back of her hand. "The opposite."

What's the opposite of pregnant? "Barren?" I guessed.

She pulled her head back then nodded, letting out another closed-eyed howl. "One of my ovaries ..." she was trying to talk through the crying, but not enough air was getting in. "Shut ... down." She cleared her throat, tried to steady herself. "There's a hormone they can test. It's not definitive. Mine's very low."

What did this all mean? How many ovaries did you need?

"It's a sign of dwindling fertility, basically," she clarified.

"But you're only thirty-four?" I pulled up her chin. "Can you look at me?"

"Hard," she said, and lowered her eyes to my chin. We'd spent so much of our first month in bed, or on a couch, retreating from the world into each other, lying around, staring into each other's eyes in rapturous disbelief.

Now she couldn't even look me in the eye. "What age did your sister start trying?" I asked. Her younger sister had just given birth to her second child.

"Twenty-five," she whispered.

"How long did it take her?"

A loud sob. "Six years. I also have severe endometriosis."

"That's bad?"

"Yes," she roared. "Anything that has a name is bad."

"Like how bad?"

"It's scarring, basically. Tissue grows where it shouldn't. Part of why I have such painful periods. No one knows anything. Knows how bad. But my gynaecologist said if I want kids, I should start now, or as soon as possible. It doesn't mean the chances are zero. Just lower. Who knows how long that last ovary will keep working?"

"Oh," I said, blinking slowly.

"I'm sorry I didn't tell you. It was wrong." Now she looked me in the eye. "I made such a big deal about the truth and that whole scene at the airport. I will never lie." She looked left and right. "This was not a lie. But it was a serious ... what's the word, omission?"

"It was kind of a lie."

The sobbing intensified. "Was it? No. You never asked about fertility stuff."

"I asked how the doctors went."

She pulled back from me. "Did you?"

"In your kitchen. You were cooking."

"Really?" She screwed her eyes closed and shook into my arms. "I'm a hypocrite. A soon-to-be barren hypocrite." Her voice rose in pitch. "And a liar."

I hugged her tighter. "No," I said. "No, no, no. It's okay." I hated seeing her suffer, but I didn't know how to help her. To make her feel good, which she claimed I was so good at. "I have lied too," I said. "Before I knew it was such a big deal to you."

The sobbing stopped. She took a deep, heaving breath and turned as I relaxed my grip so she could reach down to the floor and rummage around in her bag for a tissue. She found one and blew her nose. "About what?"

My heart raced, but then it had been racing since I'd seen the police enter our road. I wasn't exactly sure how many lies I'd told her. I'd planned to collect them up after that scene in the airport. To confess. But exploring your character flaws isn't fun, so I'd avoided it. I tried to think of the first lie. Went back to the beginning.

It didn't take long. "You know I said Annett and I broke up nine months before you and I met?"

"You're still together?" she said, gasping.

"What? No. Just, well, it was more like four months?"

77

"Oh," she said, with a heavy blink.

"Maybe I was afraid you would think I wasn't over her? But there's more. I went on a date after we met."

"When? *What?*" Another gasp. "After India?"

"It was set up before we met," I rushed to say. "A friend of a friend. I postponed it because of India, and I just, this person hadn't done anything wrong, you know?" I lifted my shoulder. "I felt like I owed it to her? And we weren't like a real thing yet."

"I see," she said, letting go of me to blow her nose. "How was it?"

"She was ..." I bit my lip. "A person? A perfectly nice person, I suppose?"

"I see," she said, as if I was finished. I wasn't finished. "And when you left me alone in your house the first time, I went through all your bedroom drawers."

She laughed, and it was a relief to hear it, to know we were closer to our normal than I had suspected. That we'd not lost it forever, buried it like Pompei, under lies.

"I did that too," she said. "I found your handcuffs. That worried me at first."

I laughed. "They're fluffy."

"Yeah, and they have a safety release catch. No murderer uses fluffy handcuffs with a safety release catch."

I remembered something else. "In India, near that giant statue thing on the coast?"

"Yeah."

"We were on the viewing platform, and you said you wanted kids. I said I wanted them too. I didn't mean it. I just wanted to sleep with you. I would have said anything."

She took her hand from my back. "You can't lie about something like that."

I covered my face with my hands. "I know."

It went quiet. We were lying down now, looking up at

the ceiling. I wanted it to be over, but sensed we were only pausing to reload. That I could find more if I looked. I didn't want to look. She was feeling better, right? Wasn't that enough?

"You finished?" she asked. "The confessions?"

I nodded. "Those're the big ones. You?"

She closed her eyes and took a deep breath. "No," she said in a quiet voice.

I let out a long, sad moan. There was already so much to process, not just from all the omission and lies, but from the fertility news. What that would mean for us.

"But this one is not a lie," she said. "Not really."

The queasy sensation returned to my stomach. It was a thin line between a lie and an omission, and she didn't seem to know where to draw it.

"I met Annett," she whispered.

"What do you mean you met Annett?" I turned and stared, my nostrils flaring.

"I met her for a drink."

"Like, by accident?" I barked.

She cleared her throat. "No, I wrote her and asked her to meet. It was the day after I got all the bad fertility news."

I scrambled away, got up off the bed. I couldn't look at her.

"I asked her not to tell you." She continued. "She's great, by the way. Really entertaining."

"That's ..." I paced back and forth on the narrow strip next to the bed. "I google-stalked your exes, or tried to, but that's not even." I waved my arms around. "I didn't even confess that because everyone does it." I was shouting now. "But I didn't ask any of them for a fucking beer." I pointed at her and flashed my teeth. "I didn't mine them for information on you. That's ... *weird*. That's ... a violation."

"Don't shout."

"I'll shout if I want. Don't you tell—"

She slid off the bed, grabbed her handbag, and ran for the door.

"Wait," I pleaded as the door thudded shut. "You can't—"

10

Hobbling out onto the terrace, I felt like I'd taken a baseball bat to the face. I sat, listening to the kids squawk and play, my insides a brooding, tangled ball of nerves and anger. Shouldn't I have been the one to run off? Not that I run off. It doesn't help. Just makes the person you flee from feel abandoned.

My leg refused to stay still; my body was certain a lion was chasing me, and it didn't understand why I wasn't running. There had been a lion, of course, a pride of them, actually, but they'd been here for the HDP. Evelyn was many things—more things and stranger things each day—but she wasn't a predator.

Usually, this view and the children's voices relaxed me, but not today. Children were part of the problem. Perhaps the entire problem. I stood up. There's nowhere to run in this city or a park worthy of the name, but I decided I could at least power walk somewhere.

As I walked, Istanbul continued its chaotic, entertaining daily business. An elderly woman pegged the washing to a line stretching across the road to her neighbour. A topless man with prodigious back hair barbecued sweet-smelling meat on his balcony. A teenager hung out of an upstairs window and threw a banger down into the street where a dozen kids played. There was a loud bang and a lot of panic. Everyone hit the street for an investigation. They found the culprit, dragged him outside by his ears, chastised and hit him on the backside, made him apologise, and dragged him back indoors by his other ear, grounded, and I don't mean emotionally. The case was closed in about four minutes; some cases are like that.

The one I was on was more complex. As I walked, I tried to understand why sudden bad fertility news would make you sneak out for a clandestine rendezvous with your new partner's ex-girlfriend. Not to mention lie, or at least omit, this for a month?

I couldn't figure it out. She needed to help me.

Swerving right down the hill, I ended up at our usual ferry port. I sent her a picture of its sign and she replied with a thumbs up emoticon and the number five, which I took to mean minutes, not fruit and veg a day, the Jackson family, or monkeys on the bed.

I passed the time groaning and scratching my cheek. Even if we got past this, if she could explain it, if we could forgive each other for our various lies and omissions— finding some new and deeper understanding of each other— there was now a ticking time bomb between us. She knew more about its fuse.

She arrived, her face blotchy, mascara lines running down her cheeks. "I was heading here too," she said. "The ferries are the best of this city."

We took the next one wherever it was going. We'd often pass an afternoon riding around on them. Finding a quiet corner on the upper deck, we sat opposite each other on the hard wooden benches, our knees grazing, close, but not too close. She looked smaller, as if she'd shrunk in the emotional wash. Maybe I did too. It was the middle of the day, so the ferry wasn't busy. I was glad few people were around to see us.

She blew her nose on a tissue.

"Do you want to start?" I asked.

"I can," she said. "But you wrote me."

After several long, composing breaths, I began. "You can't run off during an argument. It's not fair."

"And you can't shout." Her bottom lip quivered. "My dad was choleric. *Is* choleric. He would shout at my mum and throw things against the wall. I can't be with someone like that. I think maybe that's why I reacted to you shouting." She lifted her hands. "Not that you're choleric. You're not. I don't think?"

"Am I?" I wondered aloud. "No. I've never thrown anything. You j-just ..." I stammered. "You secretly went for drinks with my ex-girlfriend. That's ..." My voice rose. I took a moment to calm myself and lower it. "I feel like shouting just thinking about it."

She looked away. A boy came past, trying to sell us tea. I waved him away.

"How did your parents handle conflict?" she asked, trying to change the subject. I let her. We had time. Months of time if we needed it. "I never really saw them have any," I said. "So well, I'd say?"

"How did you and Annett argue, then?" She flinched as she said Annett's name, recognising her mistake.

"You mean you don't already know?" I said sarcastically.

She crossed her arms. "I didn't mine her, okay? It wasn't like that. I could see it at once. I need to tell you a story, for you to understand. Why I did, well ... it. We've talked a bit about my last boyfriend, Aaron. That he's a compulsive liar and stuff. I've spared you the worst. This was different from what happened with James. This relationship was serious." She cleared her throat. "I thought it was serious." She took a moment, looking out at the Bosphorus as we docked. "This is not something I enjoy talking about. I think there's, well ..." She sighed. "The last day of that relationship ... the first months were great. There were red flags, sure, like how he would never let me go to his apartment. But I gave him the benefit of every doubt. I know now that they call it love bombing."

"This is very stream of consciousness."

"Oh, sorry. I'll try." She angled her body away slightly. "It was in one of my books too, love bombing. Then it stopped, and the excuses started. He would never show up. Or be late. He cancelled like 80 per cent of the time. Those excuses grew ever more fanciful. One time when he was at mine, in the shower, and I bumped into my dresser and his wallet fell onto the ground. I shouldn't of, but his ID was staring back at me. I read the address. It wasn't in the area he said he lived. I found it odd but, you know, people move, and you don't always rush out and update your government IDs, do you?"

"I think mine is still my old address. With Annett." I scratched at my stubble. I had an inkling where this was going and I didn't like to think, first, that Evelyn had ever desired another man, any man, and second, that this man had dared mistreat her. She gripped the railings on her right, the boat jumping as it pulled away from the jetty. "There was about a month when I didn't see him at all," she said, wiping away a tear with her other hand.

I was tearing up too.

"He said he was abroad. There were all these reasons his trip kept getting extended, but none of them made sense. I remembered that address, decided one Saturday morning I'd go there."

"Can we stop a second?" I said, noticing my leg shaking again.

She had the narrow-eyed expression of someone ripping off a bandage. "Shouldn't it be me who needs a minute?"

I dried my eyes. "This is newer for me, and if someone cuts you, I bleed."

"That's ..." she said, rubbing my knee, "dramatic, but nice."

She handed me a tissue. We both took deep breaths, then she continued. "I went to that address. His name was on the bell. It killed me to do this. I'm terrible at confrontation. As you know. Or I was. I'm trying to be better with you. Anyway, somehow, I rang it." She put her head in her hands and rubbed, then peaked out at me from between her fingers. "He had a very distinctive voice, like a pitch higher than you would expect. That voice answered. I knew then it was all a lie. Every bit." She lowered her hands. "I stumbled away and collapsed against a wall. Sat on the floor, sobbing. It was relief too, not just sadness."

I lowered my head. "What an incredible, epic, gaping asshole."

"He was, yeah. But my story isn't over."

I shut my eyes. "Oh no."

"The front door opened, and a woman came out, pushing a pram. She passed me and I got a look at the baby. It had a stupid pink bow on its head. It was his daughter. I just knew. Very early in our relationship, he'd told me about a friend of his who had taken his girlfriend to the doctors for a first scan."

I flinched. "That was him?"

"I'm sure," she said, nodding. "Timing fits."

"What did you do?"

"I texted that I'd just met his daughter. And his girlfriend. And it was a shame he didn't take a walk with them or I'd have met him too."

My mouth fell open. "Shit."

"Yep. He said a bunch of lies, as usual. I realised he'd never break character. It's compulsive, his lying. He tried to call me a few times, then gave up. He was probably busy with the new baby."

"I want to kill him," I said, my hands tensing into fists.

"The pain of that moment," she said, wiping away a tear and turning to the seagull flying alongside us that was oblivious to the intensity of this moment, "was the worst of my life."

I remembered a time she'd overreacted to my forgetting to call her. It made sense now, as did her need for the truth and why she might want an honesty pact. And why she might secretly meet my ex-girlfriend, first to check that she really was an ex, and second to ask her about my character.

"I have this friend," I said, drying my eyes. "Janine. She's always the other woman. Her last boyfriend, well, not really her boyfriend." I shrugged. "He's married. She's been having an affair with him for eight years. Keeps telling herself he's about to leave his wife. Before that, it was a different married guy. Four years."

She nodded. "I know some women like that."

"I think ..." I said, beginning the sentence before I was exactly sure what I thought, "that she doesn't actually want to be tested in a real relationship. And that's why she picks unavailable men. Do you think, maybe, there might be some of that in you?"

"No," she said, without hesitation. She tucked some hair behind her ear. "No. That's not it. Not me. There are some things that feel like love, but they're more like," she said, sighing, "it's evil twin. I've mistaken them a few times. Most of the time, actually."

"Okay," I said.

"But I'm not now." She reached for my hand. "We have our moments, but what we're doing," she said with a smile, "even now, even in this really weird, intense conversation, it's still ..." she searched for the word, "*ernährend*? What's that in English?"

"Nourishing," I said, proud I was teaching her vocabulary too. I moved across to sit next to her, sliding my arm around her shoulder. She turned inwards, resting her arm on my leg and her head on my shoulder. "I wouldn't have gone to see Annett if it hadn't been for all the bad fertility news. I knew I'd need to decide on us quickly. You're an incredibly easy person to trust. Your words mean something, and you have all these deep friendships. You really helped heal a lot of this stuff. But I still find it really hard to trust. And it's not like I can ask you, because James and Aaron would have said they were trustworthy too. So, I went to see Annett. She has eight years of data about your character. I know you said you're still friends, but I figured that was just a thing people say."

"Okay," I said. "I get it."

"I met her, and it was true. Clear from her face. Her eyes. How she talked. There's still love there. I see it when you talk about her as well. Or deep respect, at least. And that's pretty miraculous. And it says a lot about you."

"It says a lot about her too," I said. "That relationship taught me so much. We did conflict well. You asked me about that, and I ducked your question, didn't I? We had the 'couple meeting' system." A connection fired. "Although, I got that from my family, now that I think about it. We used to have family meetings that worked on the same principle."

"How?"

"Any person can call a couple meeting and the other

person has to attend. The meetings last until both parties agree that understanding has been reached."

She laughed. "That sounds ripe for misuse."

"Annett tended to abuse the couple meeting system. We had a couple meeting about it."

We both laughed. The frost between us was melting. We kissed, briefly.

"What if you can't agree?" she asked.

"It gets tiring. At some point, the consensus you're both exhausted is reached and overshadows the lack of consensus about whatever led to the couple meeting."

"See, you're good at the middle. I've done the start of relationships a lot. And this is the greatest start ever, really, it is." She teared up again. "It's the rest I'm bad at."

"You're not."

She pursed her lips. "I am. Love. That's what I'm excited about. Where I need your help."

We'd never said I love you. *Did I love her?* I hadn't really thought about it. Wasn't what interested me in what we were doing. Or hadn't been what interested me, because now we were doing something different, were in a whole new relationship. One neither of us understood yet and would need to solidify from all this before we could build on it. If we wanted to build on it?

"It's still a big betrayal," I said, assuming she would know what I meant.

She exhaled slowly. "I know. And I'm sorry."

I clasped her hand. "I'm sorry too. It must have been a terrible blow to get that news. Not that I really understand it. Just that it's bad."

"I can send you some links, if you like?"

"That's more how you learn things. I'm anecdotal."

"It all just lowers the odds," she said. "Of both getting

and staying pregnant." Her voice dropped. "They're not zero, just lower and lowering."

We sat for a while. The ferry had docked again, the passengers around disembarking, being swapped for new ones. The boy came back with this tray of tea. I got us two. And some biscuits. Everywhere I looked, I could see the curves of mosques and the points of their minarets. I wished I could believe in something bigger than myself. Something with a plan for me. For us.

"Can you tell me why you want them?" I asked as the ferry narrowly missed one coming in the other direction. "I've seen you coo over them, like the little girl on the plane, but many people do that."

"I love everything about them," she said without hesitation. "That they've not learned to lie or be embarrassed. That they love and feel so ..." she went off to look for some words, returning with, "shamelessly? Everything I'm bad at, they're good at. And vice versa. Like, they can't make an Ottolenghi fig and orange salad, or talk politicians out of a rash decision, but they're also not stuck in their head, hating themselves, endlessly worrying what people think of them," she gushed. "And, well, it's the point of all this, isn't it? The point of *us*. Plus, a mix of my brains and your looks?" she said, smirking. "Come on, that would be devastating, don't you think? The world wouldn't be ready for that."

I squeezed her hand. *Was I ready for that?*

I turned my head from the spray coming now over the side of the ferry. The wind had whipped up. Sure, we'd talked about wanting kids, just as we'd talked about wanting to start a commune, live in Tribeca, write books together, and found a cult.

Talk is easy. Dreams are cheap. I hoard them in every nook of my mind. There's almost nothing I don't plan to do someday. Whether I actually do is unimportant. The empty space of possibility is what I crave. Possibility is its own reward. Doesn't need to be acted upon. Which makes life choices that reduce possibility—filling the large-yet-treasured gaps in my life and geography—really scary. Commitment costs potential and a child is the largest commitment you can make: to yourself, to your partner, to society, to the future.

It's a hell of a way to fill the day, basically. And I already filled the day easily, listening to podcasts, hunting for chocolate, and pottering around.

On this ferry, inside of me, a debate took place, or what started as a debate but became a no-rules wrestling match. On the one side was *Intellect*, an ageing professorly figure, in green tweed and a cravat, smoking his pipe. A man rational to fault and prone to both using words like pontificate and pontificating.

His opponent, *Emotion*, swirled in a circle listening to 90's power ballads, composing poetry in his mind, rubbing coke from his nose, and weeping about how AMAZING everything is—*does everyone know how amazing everything is?*

Intellect knew that there were hundreds, perhaps even thousands, of women in this world who could make me as happy as Evelyn did. That losing her would wound at first, then hurt, then sting, then nip, but would, eventually, heal.

Emotion knew little, but FELT TO HIS VERY CORE, that Evelyn was a drug whose high was unlike anything else he'd ever experienced—and he'd made it his life's work to experience. Other women were stars, sure, but she was an entire galaxy.

There was only now.

There was only her.

Emotion won the fight easily. He didn't play fair. He

didn't have to. Wasn't interested in morality, only what felt right.

She felt right.

"The lies and omissions and stuff," I said. "What does it say about us?"

"Just that we're human."

We kissed, our lips wet from the tears and phlegm. An incredible rush of intimacy. To show yourself, your worst self, and be embraced, regardless.

"This changes everything, right?" I asked.

She gave a small nod. "It does, yes."

"I need to let the beginning go, don't I?"

"If you want to be with me, yeah, I think you probably do, yes."

"I don't know if I can."

She smiled. "Go easy on yourself," she said. "It's only day one."

I laughed, and as I did, watched an idea arrive in her mind, her eyes brightening. "I know a place that might help ..."

11

Who do people think they are?

You're quietly living your day-to-day life—following tried and tested routines towards poorly defined goals you can't remember making—when these people saunter over, open a hole in their face, and casually throw words at you.

Explosive words.

BOOM! Your entire life blows up.

Once, a little more than a decade ago, in my parents' spare bedroom in Cambridge, I answered a phone. At the other end of the line, a sea away in Germany, was a skinny, ginger-haired man called Lukasz. We conversed, and it was fine enough. At the end of that conversation, he said—as if it were nothing, and to him, I suppose, it was nothing—*would you like to move to Leipzig?*

I doubt he even remembers uttering those words.

I doubt he remembers who I am.

But because of those seven words I ...

Left every friend I had.

Left my entire family.

Left my language.

Left my culture.

And left a well-paying job to move to Leipzig, a place where, until he'd said them, I didn't even know existed.

Yet—such was the power of those words—three weeks later, I stepped down from a tram outside Leipzig's city hall, schlepping a suitcase containing all the pertinent objects of my life.

None of them were shirts.

More than a decade later, I'm still living in Germany, albeit in Berlin, Leipzig's big brother.

That's the power of words, when used right. And that's why you must be careful with them. Because you can't know when you're meeting someone at a moment of heightened suggestibility, ripe for whimsy.

He wasn't even very nice, this Lukasz; he didn't have to be.

She was nice, this Evelyn (not too nice, as she feared). She was doing it too; in fact, it was all she'd done since, twenty-four hours after our lives crossed paths, she'd called me and said, "The race. India ... were you serious?"

This time it wasn't her fault, I suppose. The explosive words that had blown up her life—and by extension, my life and our relationship—had come from a gynaecologist: If you want kids, start now.

And that was annoying, really. I tried not to show my annoyance as—the day after that ferry ride—I looked up at the sign of the museum she'd brought me to on the other side of Beyoğlu.

The Museum of Innocence.

She hooked her arm into mine and yanked me inside, into a sterile room full of sad, static objects in Plexiglass boxes. She read the underwhelm on my face and handed me a headset.

"Just wait," she said, clipping it to my ear.

I walked to the first rectangular Plexiglass cabinet,

pressed one on the number pad, and promptly fell into a deep trance of story-powered reverence.

The Museum of Innocence was built by Nobel Prize-winning author, Orhan Pamuk, for his book of the same name. That book tells the story of a wealthy thirty-two-year-old called Kemal. Kemal falls in love with his eighteen-year-old distant cousin, Füsun. They have a brief affair before she breaks it off. He spends years obsessing about her, searching for her, hoarding anything she's ever touched, while going slowly insane.

He kept it all: 4213 cigarette butts pinned to boards like you might display an insect or butterfly collection, a bottle of Raki they drank together on a date, a salt shaker she touched once in a restaurant.

Each box, full of neatly arranged bric-a-brac, showed not just their failed love story but how Istanbul has changed over the decades that the novel covers. Evelyn read the book in our first week here and visited the museum a few days earlier with Leanne, a girl from her Turkish class.

"It's incredible," I said an hour later as I perched on the edge of Kemal's bed in the museum's attic. Evelyn sat down on the rocking chair opposite me. "That was really, really wonderful."

"This is where he is told the story," she said, looking around the small room. "It's just as I imagined it."

"You didn't make it up here last time?"

"No. I got tired."

"I need to read the book," I said.

Her mouth turned down. "The book is boring."

"Really?"

"Yeah. He's just really whiny and kind of creepy."

"The author?" I asked.

"Kemal, the protagonist."

Kemal had captured, trapped, and entombed an entire

beginning. Every detail. He'd become stuck in the early heady rush of infatuation, relieving the scenes of their honeymoon period. Had become obsessed with it, with her, long after she had moved on. And it had destroyed his life.

"He was in love," I said defensively.

"Pfft, he was in lust. And with a much younger girl he didn't really know."

"They probably had a special connection?"

"Weird how that special connection is always between a young woman and an older man, right?" She scoffed. "Never the other way round?"

"Er ..." my eyes danced in a circle. "I'm not a stalker. Or a predator."

"No." She shook her head. "I know. You're not that." She lowered her eyes. "That's not what I mean. Not why I brought you here. It's more about the beginning, I guess. How it's easy to get obsessed with it, because it is so wonderful." She smiled. "So intense. I wish we could have stayed in the beginning too. It was the nicest few weeks of my life, I think."

"I guess I got a longer one than you."

"Yeah," she agreed. "I guess so. And there's going to be many great times ahead," she said. "If you want them to be. If you can accept that, we have big decisions to make soon. I need your help. I don't know how to do a middle. To just be in just a normal, happy, healthy relationship. One you could even think about adding a child to."

I shivered at the word.

"But you do," she added. "If you want that again?"

I rubbed my hands together. "What does your fertility news mean exactly? How would you want to move forward? Is there another ultimatum coming?"

She straightened her blouse. "I don't believe in ultimatums, as you know," she said as a slight grin escaped her otherwise serious, professional expression.

I grinned too. "And yet," I said.

"Death or glory," she said sharply, her eyes widening.

I laughed. "I like the sound of that."

"Okay," she said. "So. Well. Argh. It's hard to sit up in a rocking chair. I should sit up. This is serious. Stupid, unserious chair." She leaned forward. "When this trip's over, it'll be July. At that point, we need to make a commitment to each other." Her words rushed out. "A promise. Not to having kids then, but that we could entertain the idea of starting a family together soon." She lifted her hand to stop me from interrupting, which I wasn't going to do. "We can do whatever you want to get you ready. Travel. Stay in Berlin. We can ..." her head tilted, "do couple's therapy? Have an orgy? Um ..." Her eyes rolled upwards. "Or run away and take DMT on a Peruvian mountaintop? Whatever you need. But in January next year, if we're still together, I want to stop being careful. By July next year, if I'm not pregnant, I want to go to a clinic and find out what we can do." She winked. "That clear enough?"

"Oh," I said, falling backwards on to Kemal's pillow and closing my eyes. A tape played scenes at fast forward from potential lives whizzing past.

"Sorry," she said, again as if she was annulling my winning lottery ticket.

A minute passed in this small room that smelt of cigarette smoke. At some point, I opened my eyes to stare up at the ceiling, whose fan span impotently. Occasionally, during that minute, several words reached my lips before crumbling away. Not explosive words, just calm, intelligent, erudite ones that would have nudged things forward. Things needed to be nudged forward. I could nudge them forward, couldn't I? She was waiting.

I sat up and, hoping for the best, opened my mouth. It hung there for a while and I almost closed it again, but then, after a short gurgling noise, I squeezed out, "So this is, like, a lot?"

"Yeah," she said. "I suppose it is."

12

On the way home, we stopped at a cafe that specialised in novelty sodas—as if my insides weren't already fizzy enough. I spent a lot of the walk rubbing parts of myself, trying to release tension.

Evelyn's steps were lighter, as if she'd removed a heavy anvil of worry from around her neck. I was now part of her devilish conspiracy. She had told me things—achingly personal and deeply embarrassing things. She'd revealed lies and omissions and traumas and hopes and dizzying, terrifying, potential relationship timelines, yet I was still here, sitting with her at a small, rickety wooden table, stroking her leg with my foot, waiting for her to remember she was drinking my half of our impossibly delicious, plum and ginger soda.

The next move was mine; I knew. She had set the time-line. Had even named the project (Death or Glory); I just had to agree to it. *Did I agree?*

"I mean," I said, but faded out.

She looked up from the magazine she'd found about notable people caught doing mundane things without makeup. "Yes?" she asked.

"I suppose ..." I said, fading out again.

She blinked several times. "Hmm?"

A waitress stopped by to clear the table next to us. I watched her, waiting until she'd left. "We don't need to decide anything now, right? The next decision is when the trip ends?"

Her mouth narrowed. "Yeah, I suppose so?"

"The holiday is the first test."

She lifted her hands. "That's what I've been saying."

"Yeah." I pushed out my lips. "Well, I guess now I'm saying it too? Since I now know it's a test? And what we're being tested for?"

"It's just a human." She shrugged. "Or maybe two?"

We laughed. It was nice to laugh together. Not as nice as that soda, but nice.

"How about a change of scenery, then?" I asked with a small wiggle of my hips. "Mix things up? Why don't we go to Hemin's village in Kurdistan? Istanbul's annoying me."

"I'm not sure there's much there other than, you know, goats," she said, before taking the last, loud, gurgling sucks of MY SODA. "Delicious," she said, putting it down, empty. "But we could go to Mardin and Diyarbakir? That would be really interesting."

"Is it safe enough?" I pulled out my phone. "Let me check the British Home Office website."

I read the first two lines. I stopped reading. "They'd warn you not to go to the local park. What about the German Foreign Office?"

She laughed. "They put the whole of Turkey on the no-go list weeks ago when they locked up those aid workers and tourists. German tourism's down 90 per cent but," she said, tilting her head, "I'll check with Hemin."

A minute later, her phone vibrated with an answer. "He says it's fine. Has friends we can visit."

I steepled my hands. "Did he mention anything about taking up arms while we're there?"

"Nope." A seagull landed on a nearby railing, sitting there happily until a child chased it away. As metaphors went, it was very on the nose.

"It would help us understand him better," she said. We were a decisive pair, in our best moments, and we dived into flight research as a smell of coffee wafted out from the cafe's kitchen. I had a startling realisation: of all the world's available men, Evelyn had hung her reproductive hat on me.

Me.

As opposed to an actual man: someone who owned power tools, knew what a spark plug was, had a signature BBQ sauce glaze, could grow a dictator's beard, name more than a dozen vegetables, and drank coffee.

I stood up abruptly. The empty bottle wobbled. "I'm going to order a coffee."

"You don't like coffee."

"Let's see," I said.

I returned with a small cup, hand-painted with a purple cat. "Every other adult seems to like coffee." I sat down. "Must be something to it." I brought the steaming brew up to my thirsting lips. Lips thirsting not for coffee, but knowledge, and I suppose, perhaps, masculine respectability?

I took a tentative sip. I spat. "Yuck. Why's it so bitter?"

She nodded sagely. "Yep, that's coffee."

"How did this drink take over the world?"

"The smell is incredible, no?"

I held it under my large, bulbous nose and sniffed. "Okay, that's pretty good. Earthy. And hmm ... coffee-ish? What coffee is this?"

She tilted the cup in her direction. "Espresso, I'd say?"

"Maybe I'm more of a mocha?"

"Do you even know what a mocha is?"

"The milky one?"

"How have you lived this long, yet learned so little?"

I put the cup down. "I've a real knack for ignorance."

"This about the kid thing?" she asked, nodding at the cup.

I shrugged. "I'd just be a kid, having a kid."

"Don't you think that's how everyone feels?"

"Yes," I said. "But those people are wrong. I'm actually, genuinely, massively, an immature idiot. I don't even know what a ..." my eyes darted around, "spark plug is?"

She shrugged. "Neither do I. Is that a thing you need to know?"

"I don't know? Yeah? Maybe, like, the kid is dying and the only thing that will save it is a spark plug and then we can't find it because we don't know what it is and the kid is dead now, and that's on us?"

She pursed her lips. "I'm pretty sure it's a car thing."

"I've never even owned a car," I said as she finished my espresso. I mean, just the cheek of it. Of her.

"Neither have I," she said.

I wanted to punish her for several things, most recently that she'd drunk two of my drinks, even if one was just hot mud, and so I said, "I'm going to cook for us tonight. On my own. And not following a recipe."

* * *

"I always feel like an idiot because I don't know the names of things. Real men know the names of things," I said, at the twenty-four-hour supermarket next to our apartment. We were standing side by side before a wall of green bins over-loaded with fruits, vegetables, and nuts. I'd found a recipe on the walk: a spinach, basil, and plum salad. It sounded difficult. I wanted it to be difficult.

I pointed to a small, bruised, purple and green wrinkled sack. "What is the name of that?"

Evelyn scanned my face, looking for signs I was joking. "You aren't joking, are you?"

"Nope."

"It's a fig," she said, with the 1+1=2 tone of a patient primary school teacher. I repeated the word. "*Fig*. I've heard of those."

"You've never tried a fig?"

"Dunno."

"They're amazing. Get some figs."

We got figs. We got several things.

The customer is king of Istanbul. If you even casually glance at a fig or, well, anything at all, one of the enthusiastic sales boys will magic six of them into a plastic bag before you've had time to blink. If you take it, they add four more bags with things you didn't have time to glance at yet but go really well with the thing you did. A nut's shoved in your mouth. Tea is poured down your neck. Honey is dripped in your ear. A best price you are promised. Return often, you are told. A good day to you is wished. They extracted money from your wallet, half as much as you expect.

"What are these?" I asked, pointing to the thing next to the figs. We were on a fruit roll now, assuming figs are fruit.

"A different type of fig," she said.

We had rolled into a wall. A wall of figs.

"There's more than one type of fig?"

She let out a moan. "There's more than one type of fig."

"I didn't really eat fruit or vegetables until my twenties," I explained. "I was nineteen when I first tried a strawberry. True story."

"Sad story. What *did* you eat growing up?"

"Chocolate."

102

I looked down at the full containers of assorted, unlabelled green things. I needed spinach for my recipe, and I was pretty sure it was in the extended lettuce-patchwork family.

"Spinach ... Spinach ... Spinach ..." I mumbled.

Her hands were on her hips. "Are you telling me you don't know what spinach is?"

"I know Popeye ate it?"

"Who the hell is Popeye?"

"Sailor man."

"Do you mean a sailor?" she asked.

"He might not have made it to Germany. You're a bit landlocked."

"We have a sea."

"Barely."

The fruit and veg man waited patiently, listening to us, an open, striped bag in his hands, primed and ready to unspool more if needed, like ammo in the war I was fighting against my many inadequacies. Food and I have always had a very simple, functional relationship. I viewed it purely as a way out of the prison of hunger. But this was not how normal people approached food, nor how Evelyn approached it. She read cookbooks for fun of an evening, curled up on the couch, foaming at the edges of her mouth. Her spice rack's real estate was as contested as downtown San Francisco. Near that spice rack were *two* pestles and mortars.

I had learned the word from her: pestle and mortar.

She reached out and tapped some dark, wide green leaves; the boy bagged a bunch, shaking the water off. "Spinach," she said as I stepped back from the fruit and vegetables, deciding I'd done enough damage to my reputation. I sidestepped to the bins of nuts; I'm knowledgeable about nuts. Or rather, about peanuts: Emperor Nut.

"Should I get some peanuts?" I asked confidently, drawing attention to them with a flourish of my open hand.

"Of all the multitudes of possible nuts, your suggestion is peanuts?"

"Peanuts are good. Salty."

She frowned. "But are they pistachio good? Are they honeyed-cashew good?"

"Pistachio ..." I said exuberantly. "It sounds like what a magician would shout before sawing a woman in half."

"Hmm ..." she said.

"I've only ever had it as ice cream."

She sighed. "Right, and where do you think the pistachio in the ice cream comes from?"

"The ice cream factory?"

"They come from these." She ran her hand through a bin of small, brown, unshelled nuts.

"Do you have to shell them?" I asked, my voice thick with disdain. "Because you don't have to shell peanuts."

She stared.

She blinked.

She blinked.

She blinked. "You know you have to shell peanuts, right?"

I puffed out my chest. "I've never shelled one."

"Yeah, that's because *other* people are shelling them for you."

"Really? Well, can those people not shell the pistachios for me as well, then?"

"Are you short of time?"

"Not really, I guess?" I put some pistachios in a bag. Or rather, tried to, but the boy leapt between me and them, scooping them in for me. We paid and left, our limbs draped in striped bags of produce. It cost basically nothing. The lira really was in the toilet. Andrea was right.

"I'm good at carrying though," I said, trying to win back respectability points—for I am a bulky, generously proportioned man with giant bucket hands, wide and flat shoulders, and the biggest calves in the Western hemisphere. "You could load me up like a huge, bald donkey, and I'd plod down the road without complaint. Well, with perhaps minimal complaint."

"We live next door," she said, because in a day in which she'd already taken so much from me—emotionally, physically, future-ly—she couldn't even give me this one tiny, weird compliment about my calves. No, not even that. That was too much for her, too.

I groaned, and not from the weight of our figs and spinach. "Let's book some damn flights."

13

On the sanctuary of our terrace, under the shade I had installed using a whole roll of sellotape, we speared at the leaves of the salad I had started, became confused and over-whelmed by, ruined, then ran from the kitchen leaving her to save.

My phone rang; it was Nick, a friend from Berlin who I'd travelled to South Africa with, perhaps a year earlier.

"How's the kid?" I asked when the video call connected. He had a four-month-old son I'd only met a few times, and who had always been asleep. Nick's eyes darted left and right. "Cracking. Yeah." I waited for him to hold up a newspaper with today's date. "What's that in the back-ground?" he asked.

"Tarlabaşı."

He whistled. "Terrific."

"Sure is. Everything okay with you and Antje?"

He also had a German partner he'd met in a bar. "Sure. Sure. *Fine.*"

"We just booked a flight to Mardin," I said, and his face illuminated, revealing the old wanderlust Nick, the great hemisphere rambler, a man I'd never believed could settle down, stay in one place, have a family. "I've always wanted to go to bloody Mardin," he said, his voice tinged with jealousy.

"So come with us?" I offered nonchalantly, because they were just words, right? The first words came to me. And what are words? Nothing. You can throw them at people and it's fine.

"Well," he said. "Funny you should say that, because that's why I called. Antje's taking the boy on a family holiday to the Baltic Sea. I'm not much use these days. He's boob obsessed, the lad, and there will be enough grandparents around. I was thinking about getting away myself, like."

"We're also going to Diyarbakir."

He licked his lips. "Even better."

Evelyn had moved inside to give me some privacy. I found her huddled over her phone, doing her Turkish flashcards, cramming for an end-of-semester test. How many times had she met Nick? Three, at most?

She looked up at me, looming over her. "Did you know Turkish has a tense just for gossip?"

I crouched. "Seriously?"

"For making it clear you got the knowledge second-hand, so don't know if it can be relied upon."

"Do you know that for sure, or did you just hear it from someone?"

She laughed. "What can I do for you?"

"You know how you like Nick, right?"

"He's kind of intense."

"Nick's coming with us to Kurdistan."

"What?" She tipped back her head. "Why?"

Ha, take that!

I'm doing it to you!

Destroying your plans.

How does it feel? Shit, right? Shit.

I cleared my throat, trying to keep my voice neutral. "It just happened. I mentioned it and, well, he leapt on it, and almost against my will, I was forwarding him our flight confirmations. It's not his style, discussion. He does things and those around him must react. If he doesn't like the reaction, he wanders wordlessly off. He's a cat, basically, but a cat that's read lots of *Economist* articles and so has terrific conversational range."

She stared at me. She said nothing.

"And, I mean, we're discussing it now?"

"You're not just telling me?" she asked as I felt an already snug noose tighten. "There are some aspects of telling, that's true, but that could be a precursor to discussion, right? And, you know, an interesting time for him. He's just had a baby. We can see how that's going for them? How he and Antje have adjusted? They weren't together two minutes before she got pregnant. I think they were on acid at the time."

"What's he like to travel with?" she asked.

I swatted the air. "Fine. Totally fine. As long as he gets to make *all* the decisions."

14

A VERY BRIEF HISTORY OF THE KURDS

Imagine you're at a relaxing board game evening with your friends, David, Georges, and Woodrow, and sat around the large pine table in your living room. Crisps are being eaten and you're all sipping from cold beers made warm by friendship. You raise your bottles and chink. Against everyone's better judgement, you decide to play the tabletop strategy game Risk.

The game starts with light cavalry sparring in South America and Australasia, as everyone decides their strategies, grabs land, and spreads out. You take up a position in the Middle East, deciding it will be your power base. It's central, and from it, if you make the right allies, you could march out into Europe, Asia, perhaps even Africa?

You feel good about what you are building. You call your people Kurds, believed to be an ancient word for nomad.

Nature calls. You answer. It takes longer in there than you expect. You really should eat more fibre, but you get the job done. You return, sit down, look down at the board, your mouth falls open, and you scream.

Everything has changed.

You're told that, while you were away, an archbishop's been assassinated, and things escalated into a kind of Great War-type debacle. Everyone's sorry they couldn't wait for you, but world history doesn't work like that. There are long periods where nothing happens, then everything happens all at once.

Everything has happened all at once.

In your absence, your so-called friends, David Lloyd George, Georges Clemenceau, and Woodrow Wilson have strategised against you, making pacts and treaties, deciding to requisition some of your oil-rich Middle Eastern positions for themselves. In the process, they've also redrawn a few borders, creating a new country or two.

Iraq, for example.

But it's not fair, you shout.

Yes, they say, but what is? This isn't about fairness, it's about power, resources, politics. It's about Risk.

You stare forlornly down at your former territory. At your people. At the culture that was fermenting amongst them. They still live where they used to, but rather than being united, these geographic changes split them into four small parts in what's now calling itself: Iran, Syria, Iraq, and Turkey.

Your Kurds are a minority in each. *It won't work*, you protest, waving your arms around—my people differ from those that now govern them. They are not Arabs, Persians, or Turks: they're Kurds. They speak an Indo-European language. Sure, most are Muslim, but a different, more liberal Muslim. Their culture, beliefs, identity, language— they're distinct, proud, and now they will be subsumed.

You ask for changes but you've no allies. Everyone avoids eye contact with you. The game advances. There's a huge spat brewing between America and the USSR.

Communism is on the rise. There are bigger political fish to fry than you and your Kurds.

The years pass. Games of Risk are endless. You sit, taking your turn when the dice are given, rolling, plotting, planning, hoping, but knowing you've lost. There are simply no good moves you can make.

Your Kurds try everything anyway: in 1919, pulling off an uprising in Iran under famed Kurdish leader Sheikh Mahmoud Hafid Barzanji and even a short-lived Kurdish kingdom in 1922, crushed in 1924. This uprising damages your reputation, and the rulers of the four countries your people find themselves in grow first weary, then outright hostile towards your people.

A hundred game years pass with them still subjugated and divided. You are the world's largest stateless group. In Syria (two million Kurds), you are perennially second-class citizens. In Iran (eight million Kurds), you are 10 per cent of the population but have almost none of its power. Your politicians are regularly imprisoned or executed. In Iraq (five million Kurds), Saddam Hussein and his Ba'ath Party ruthlessly persecute you, using chemical weapons, murdering over 180,000 of you, in what is now considered an attempted genocide.

I am sorry.

Turkey, where the majority of your people live (twenty million Kurds), deny your culture exists, until recently calling you Mountain Turks or Easterners (Doğulu), as well as arresting your politicians and banning your language for decades. In response, the Kurdish Worker's Party (PKK), a radical leftist organisation, is founded—the USA calls it a terrorist organisation—and it attacks the Turkish state in a long, bitter fight for autonomy. A fight that has never really ended.

The game continues. The decades pass. Europe and the

USA dominate the map for decades, but now Asia ascends. No one bothers giving you the dice anymore. Still you wait, still you hope, still you dream of your own state. Because it's not a game to you, it's about fundamental rights: to your own borders, your own rules, your own language; to see your people united again in the simple joy and cushioned safety of being a majority.

Today, that dream is most alive in northern Iraq, where the disastrous US-led war creates a leadership vacuum your people fill admirably. The Kurdish Democratic Party (HDP) is the dominant party of Iraqi Kurdistan, and its Kurdistan Regional Government (KRG) administers it—a progressive place where 16 per cent of the GDP is spent on education and women make up 40 per cent of the military and 30 per cent of the government.

It's something, but it's not enough. And if things haven't changed in this long, they're unlikely to soon. Kurds have no friends but the mountains, your people like to say, and who would dare disagree with them?

15

We waited at the arrivals gate of Mardin Airport. It had been a full minute since Evelyn had said anything. "Did I tell you about that car crash when I was here last?" she asked, ending it.

I nodded. "Like three times."

"Really?"

"You told me on the plane to India already."

"Huh. How about the one in Lagos where the car broke down in the middle of the night?"

"Yep. Another good one."

She looked down, disappointed.

The door parted and Nick sauntered through, sports holdall thrown over his shoulder, back arched, head up, looking around with his trademark slightly miffed expression, wondering why a trumpet player had not announced his arrival.

I waved, and he strode over. "No sign? No rose?"

We were just about the only people at the airport. Seven kilometres away, a civil war was raging in Syria. Tourism was not so much in the toilet as down in the deepest depths of the sewer.

"Hi Nick," Evelyn said. "How was—"

He whistled. "Look at you two, all sun kissed. Istanbul has been kind. Too kind, some might say?"

I grabbed at the new flab around my stomach. "It's her cooking."

"And there's nowhere to run," she said. Her eyes darted left and right. "That's not a threat."

"How was your flight?"

"Magic," he said. "Empty. No babies. All the sleep I wanted. Right." He gestured off towards the nearest door. "Let's go then."

We skipped along the other side of the barrier after him. "Why don't we get a coffee first and catch up? I want to hear more about fatherhood."

He waved me off. "No time for that old guff. And you don't even like coffee."

"That's not true," I said. "No, it is true. But I'm trying to change. I'm doing a bit of an adulthood project."

"He also knows the name of eight vegetables now," Evelyn said in a tone that couldn't decide between pride and ridicule.

"We can get coffee in town," he said, heading for the nearest door. "We've an ancient city to explore."

"Does he even know where he's going?" Evelyn whispered as we scampered after him.

"That won't stop him."

The doors parted, and we stepped out, smashing straight into a thick wall of heat that blew us backwards.

"I finally made it to Mardin," he said, sucking in a lungful of the soupy air. "Just look at her. What a stunner."

We stared up at a city cut into the top of a mountain, shimmering in the heat haze.

He darted towards the nearest bus stop. "I read about a little place we can stay. Great reviews."

Evelyn tried to keep up. "I know somewhere too. It's where the politicians and dignitaries stay. It's cut right into the rock. I stayed there last time. It's like—"

He stopped dead. His head turning back slowly. "You've been here before?"

"Yes."

His smile collapsed. It would be difficult to pretend he knew more about a place he'd never been to than someone who had both been there and was always exquisitely well researched. He rebuilt his smile. "These reviews," he said with a whistle.

"Mine's an old castle," she countered.

"Well, mine has a dog."

"That's ..." she faltered.

A bus was waiting. Nick got on that bus without asking where it was going. "Why don't we do one night at—" Evelyn suggested.

"Faff," he said, as I remembered my rule about not travelling as a three. My phone informed me it was 41 °C. "It is hot to move twice," I said, realising with regret that I had the deciding vote. Evelyn was almost certainly more prepared, and also right, but Nick was less reasonable and so wouldn't forgive being overruled. "Why don't we have a look at Nick's place, since it's an unknown entity? If we don't fancy it, we do your place?" I offered as we took our seats.

"That's—" she began to say.

"Deal," Nick said.

The bus pulled out onto the empty motorway. "You could have backed me up," she muttered. "My place is spectacular."

"Maybe his is too?"

"We'll go to mine for a drink and you'll see."

The bus began its ascent to Mardin, a city built high on the slopes of the Mazi Mountains. A place first settled twelve thousand years ago, and that has hosted a revolving cast of Assyrians, Romans, Muslims, Mongols, Catholics, Armenians, and Chaldeans.

I understood why they had picked this spot. The altitude helped a little with the heat; we were on the only raised surface as far as the eye could see, so this was a place you could protect; and the view didn't hurt. You could see across the plains almost all the way to Syria.

The bus dropped at the far end of town, nearer Nick's accommodation. "It's just up here," he said, striding up the first alley he saw. Mardin is a city of narrow passageways designed to maximise shade. The buildings, many made of yellow limestone—and cool to the touch despite the incredible, invasive, oppressive heat—densely packed and forming what was, justifiably, a UNESCO World Heritage site.

"Are we lost?" Evelyn asked, ten minutes later, as we took a quick break on a low wall that had been a high wall before collapsing upon itself, which I was close to doing too.

"Never," he said.

More by luck than judgement, he found a discoloured sign taped to a humble wooden door near some trash bags at the end of another tight passageway.

"This is—" Evelyn said, making no effort to hide her scorn.

"Going to be great," Nick said, knocking.

Nothing happened.

Nick knocked louder.

Nothing happened again.

"Oh well, let's go to my place," said Evelyn, taking two steps from the door back the way we'd come. Nick knocked like he wanted to knock the door down. A dog barked and growled. Nick turned, his eyebrows bouncing. "That'll be the dog then."

"Do you even like dogs?" I asked.

"Depends on the dog."

The door opened a slither.

"Merhaba," said half of a woman's face, visible through a narrow gap kept small to block a tiny, yapping dog from escaping.

"Room?" she asked.

"Bingo," said Nick. "I mean, yes, I mean, *please*?"

The austere entrance gave no clue to the oasis hiding beyond it: a beautiful, tiled, square courtyard and three-storey building chiselled directly into the rock.

"One hundred years old," the woman said proudly, as if she'd built it.

"Just a hundred?" Evelyn mumbled. "Mine is at least three hundred."

"Cracking," said Nick before we'd even passed the threshold. "Two nights please."

We followed the woman to reception, followed, in turn, by the source of all the growling and barking: a tiny, long-hair black dog with a squashed grape face. He had a pronounced underbite and bulbous, over-sized eyes set in a head two sizes too small. To say he had a face only a mother could love would be a stark exaggeration of the maternal bond.

Because of all that hair, wherever he walked, he mopped.

"Lucky," said the woman, looking down at him adoringly.

No, he's not, I thought.

The woman led us inside, where, to our great relief, it was cold. I hugged the walls. "Very old," said the lady in German, the only language we had in common. "You like? Very difficult. I buy hotel three years ago, but since the war, no tourists come to Mardin."

She left us alone to get settled. "Nice place, huh?" I said.

Evelyn frowned. "I guess."

"Yours is nicer?"

She laughed, unzipped her backpack, tipping the contents all over the bed. "I thought you'd have been on my side," she said. "About the accommodation?"

"I don't want to be on anyone's side."

"We're travelling as a three; it's side-y," she said.

"I hate travelling as a three."

"You let it happen."

"Everyone's just doing things to me, Evelyn. You, him ..." I tried to think of other people doing things to me. "Really just you and him. But that's enough. That's already a lot."

"Poor you," she said, her voice dripping with sarcasm.

I wandered back out to the courtyard and, on its upper level, spied an empty maroon-red hammock. Only one thing separated me from it: Lucky.

The courtyard's garden was at two different heights, a raised central area with tables and chairs and hammocks, perhaps half a metre higher than the lower path that curved around it and led to reception.

Lucky was standing guard at the stairs, his woefully inadequate, stubby legs unable to climb them. He was too small to even navigate the area they ostensibly employed him to guard. I wasn't sure what came first: his personality or the conditions for it. It was a chicken and egg ... *oh*.

As I approached, he reared back up like a snake, swirling in a circle, snapping his jaws.

"Lucky," I said, bending down to stroke him. "You're not intimidating anyone, mate."

He kept trying anyway. I walked up the stairs, and the

hammock welcomed me, wrapping me in a soft embrace. I put my hands behind my head and murmured gleefully.

"Hello, Lucky," said Nick, sauntering down the path, hands in his pockets. "You're a boisterous little turd, aren't you?" He turned to me. "You awake in there, dipshit?"

"Lucky has seen to that."

"Lovely, isn't he?"

I rolled over so I could see him better. "A treasure."

"Nice digs though, aye? Worth the walk for sure. Shall we go explore the city?"

"Didn't we do that already?"

"That was alleyways, mostly."

"It seems like it is mostly alleyways? And it's too hot for exploring."

"Naaaaaah," he said, "it's fine."

"What about that coffee and catch up you promised me?"

"Plenty of time for that."

"Why don't we use some of it?" I asked.

"I can hear about your latest batch of sad neuroses in Berlin. This is a place I've always wanted to come, and they'll blow it up before I ever come here again."

"It's forty-one degrees."

Fed up with being ignored, Lucky sat down and whined softly.

"Put on sunscreen then, pillock."

"Where do you even want to go?" I asked.

"I read about this monastery nearby. It's three hundred years old."

"Does that make it better or worse?"

He tutted. "Better, of course."

"I don't know why everyone is so into the past? It seems so smallpox-y, you know? All that pointless toiling and saving potato harvest money to buy a lead-lined hat."

"I forgot what travelling with you is like." He sighed. "Where's your woman at?"

"Showering, I think?"

He made a click, click sound with the corner of his mouth, as if I was a goat he was encouraging down a mountain pass. "Let's take a taxi and check it out."

A door closed above us, and Evelyn appeared at a railing. "What's the plan, Batman? *Batmen*?"

"We're going to a monastery," Nick said.

"Nick's going," I corrected.

"Maybe I want to go to the monastery?" she said.

"It's three hundred years old," Nick enthused. Evelyn walked down to the path, fanning herself with her hat. Lucky didn't bark at her, just let her walk right past and up to my hammock. "I'm melting," she said. "I'm not built for this heat."

"No one's built for this heat," I said.

She spotted a free hammock. "You do the monastery, Nick, and when you get back, it'll be cooler and we can—"

"Dinner and drinks," Nick interrupted.

"Deal," I said, happy we were finally speaking my language. Nick left and as the sun found both hammocks, we swapped to chairs in the shade of a pear tree, Evelyn talking a lot, as usual.

"He interrupts me," she said after our fourth bottle of water. "Have you noticed? You must have noticed."

I leaned forward. "Does he?"

"Guys do it a lot."

"I'm sure they don't."

She frowned. "Why would I make that up?"

"He never does it to me, though?"

"He knows you better." She shrugged. "And you're a guy."

I tutted. "Not everything is about gender."

"This is. Should I say something to him?"

"I could?" I offered.

"But you don't believe there's a problem." She nibbled on her lip. "How do you think he would react if I mentioned it?"

I considered it. "Badly." I reconsidered it. "No, very badly."

16

Nick returned two hours later, and with the sun in retreat, we set out to discover more of the city. Freed of any particular goal or destination, we ambled down the narrow, twisting cobblestone lanes, so narrow we were often in single file, Nick at the front.

It's an understatement to say that we attracted attention. Everywhere we went, people invited us to nearby places: someone's garden, a tea shop, into an apartment, the back room of a copper engraving business. We rarely shared a language with the people trying to host, but they all had something they wanted to share: a culture, home, son studying in the USA, daughter in Amsterdam, nephew in Canada, cat.

I couldn't believe we were in the same country as frenetic, people-pressure-cooker Istanbul. The best travel is time travel. In Mardin, we'd gone back a hundred years.

"That's it," said Evelyn, pointing to a grand, tall building with turrets.

We entered its large, imposing lobby, passed two knights in armour and climbed upstairs to the first of several terraces, all of which offered sweeping, uninterrupted desert views.

"Nice enough," Nick said, sitting down.

"Nice enough?" I scoffed. "This place is spectacular."

He looked at the menu, flipped it over, stuck out his tongue, dropped the menu on the table as if offended, and said, "It doesn't have a Lucky though, does it?"

A large, chocolate-brown Labrador ambled out of the open double doors behind us and sat between two large potted plants, dropping its head between its paws, its coat shining.

Nick ignored it.

"It's special here, isn't it?" I said. "Mardin."

"I've got a bad feeling about it, though," he said.

Evelyn pointed towards Syria. "It's too near—"

"We're here," Nick said, "so it can't be that bad."

If this city was located almost anywhere else, it would be inundated with tourist buses. In these troubled times, its only regular visitors were Syrian refugees. A 100,000 had not only visited but settled in and around the city, peacefully, it seemed.

I tapped the arms of my wooden throne of a chair. "Sometimes old shit is better."

"Profound," said Nick. The waiter arrived. Nick asked for beer and the waiter shook his head and apologised several times before bowing several more in a strategic, awkward retreat.

"I bring better," he said ominously.

"Everything good with Antje?" I asked, feigning casualness.

"Sure," he replied too quickly. Evelyn and I swapped looks of intrigue. He noticed. "*It is.* Really. I know you think because it happened so fast and accidentally, it's probably not going to work, but, well, it's working fine."

"Great," I said.

"Great," he agreed, rubbing his hands together. "Topic closed."

"Did you always—" Evelyn asked, trying to reopen it.

"Can't a man just drink in a view and ponder civilisations past without an inquisition?"

She shifted in her seat. "I'm sure you don't mean to do it," she said, "but I've noticed you interrupt me sometimes?"

He froze. "Do I?"

"Quite often—"

"I'm sure," he stopped, realising he'd done it again. While I braced for his face to flash in anger, or to fire some pithy, sarcastic retort, he said, "I apologise. I won't do it again."

"Thank you," she said. "It's easily done."

I watched on in awe. First at her and how she wasn't shying away from conflict anymore, unlike in the stories she told me. Second, at him—he was not a reasonable man, which was fine. I wasn't in a dependent relationship with him. I kept him around for his interestingness. Yet, here he was, accepting criticism and apologising, vowing to change, which was proof he already had.

They both had. So I could then too, couldn't I?

The waiter returned with menengiç coffee, a milky drink made from roasted (shelled) pistachio seeds which is twice as delicious as it sounds. We moved on to sweet Assyrian wine he promised were from local grapes.

"You can ask your questions now," Nick said, his tongue loosened by those grapes. "I can see you have your question face on, Adam."

"I don't know what that means, buddy?"

"Yeah, you do."

"Oh, come on," I said. "Isn't it interesting when a close friend who never managed more than about a long weekend of monogamy, and showed no interest in kids, one-eighties on all his values and becomes a domesticated dad?"

"Uh-huh," he said, chuckling. "It's not that big of a deal. Every goon does it."

"What's a goon?" Evelyn asked.

"It's like an idiot," I said.

"How long had you been dating?" Evelyn asked. "Before, you know ..."

He waited to answer, checking she'd fully completed her sentence.

"A few weeks, maybe?" He lifted his palms. "I know, I know. Use a condom, Nick."

We laughed.

"But actually, it's working fine. We had little relationship to break, you know? There's probably less ..." he looked for the word, "pressure? When you have a bad day, there isn't all this guilt and sadness because, well, you chose this person who you thought was your soulmate, and all that guff and yet, they're not making you happy. Circumstance threw us together, Antje and I. We made Matthew, and he's bloody terrific. Now there's a special bond between us, because no one on earth will ever care for the boy like we will."

"That's lovely," Evelyn said.

"It is," I agreed.

He finished his wine and signalled for another. "It's just different from how most people do it."

"It's more like an arranged marriage," Evelyn said, carefully, unsure if it was offensive.

He nodded. "It was a bloody shock, though. I was talking to my friend Tanya about that the other week. She said this was the only way it could happen for me, because of my commitment issues."

"She's right," I said.

He shrugged. "So, it happened like this. I mean ..." his teeth scraped his lip. "I'm making it sound easy. It wasn't easy. I struggled with it for a long time. Trying to frame it positively. Not as failure, or a disaster, or being trapped."

I murmured in agreement. I knew that feeling, or a miniature version of it. I was living in it. The trap was different, more expansive, and Evelyn was in it with me. She was not my jailer, although sometimes I struggled to see it that way.

"So, what has surprised you most about it?" I asked as he ripped at a piece of bread.

"That's a typical new parent question. Not a one-thing experience, kids. There isn't a dominant emotion, other than maybe fear? It's just everything all the time—good, bad, easy, boring, hard, exciting, dull, joyous, hateful. Amazing how many emotions you can feel at once. I mean, it's also really hard, but hard is not a synonym for bad, you know?"

"Huh." I crossed my arms.

"You like that, do you?"

I nodded.

* * *

Back in the hotel, exhausted from the heat, I tried to get into bed but found my side blocked with Evelyn's ... well, everything.

"Can you not spread your stuff all over the bed?"

"Why not?" she asked.

"I want to lie there."

"So move it?"

"It's just a stupid place, you know? It has to be in the way, because we will definitely need the bed."

"It's the biggest surface, though," she said defensively.

"We're only here two nights. Do you need to unpack everything?"

"Otherwise I can't find anything."

"Systems?"

She rolled her eyes. "It's easy to have systems when you're a guy."

"Not everything is about gender."

"Toiletries are. Clothes are."

I pushed all her stuff into a small, pleasing pile and lifted it over to her side. *How had I not noticed her spreading?* "It was a nice evening," I said as we settled into bed.

"He took it well," she said. "The interruption thing."

"Yeah, I was wrong. He seems ... different?"

"Maybe," she said, and we lay and read our Kindles, or pretended to. I pretended to because I was thinking about someone else. That person barked. I sat up. "What if it was a Lucky?" I said.

"A what?"

"A Lucky?"

"If what's a Lucky?"

"Our kid. What if it got, like, my looks, my posture, my enormous nose, my tiny ears, my puny, non-dictatorial hair? What if it was the worst mix of us both?"

She sat up and kissed me on the lips, minty fresh from toothpaste. "But imagine it gets your creativity, your humour, your imagination, your way with words ..." She sped up. "Your calmness, your height, your big, sparkling brown eyes, your ability not to sweat, your calves?"

"My calves!" *I slapped my forehead.* "It's a nightmare to find trousers."

"In the Middle Ages, men actually wore padded socks to enlarge the size of their calves," she said. "Did you know that? Big calves were a real turn-on?" She patted me on the shoulder. "You were born five hundred years too late."

"I missed smallpox though, didn't I? And lead-lined hats."

"It won't be a Lucky," she said. "It will be lucky. And we'd love it anyway. Now go to sleep. It's Diyarbakır tomorrow, and that's going to be intense."

17

"I can't believe I'm actually going to Diyarbakır," said Nick the following morning in the hotel courtyard, the heat already past stifling, as he spread lashes of sickly, golden-brown honey on his bread.

At a nearby window, a hairy sausage with a face barked and growled and limbered up for another day of being obnoxious.

"Shut it, Lucky," I shouted.

"You suck," said Nick.

"Poor little guy," said Evelyn.

"It's one of those places you read about in the *Economist*," Nick continued. "Like Zanzibar or Timbuktu. Have you been there, Evelyn?"

"No. It's not been safe enough to take my politicians lately."

A small smile formed at the edges of his mouth.

If, by some miracle, the Kurds unlock all the padlocks of their geography, Diyarbakır, a Kurdish majority city—on the banks of the Tigris River and long important for its strategic location, linking the trades routes of Mesopotamia and Anatolia—will be Kurdistan's beating heart.

Because of its revered status for Kurds, it's a fractious place, a barometer of wider relations between them and the Turks.

When the going's good, Diyarbakır is calm. But when Erdoğan wants to punish them for a PKK attack or some other perceived slight, he drops his fist onto the city and its already significant military presence of roadblocks, lock-downs, and city-wide curfews intensify.

For a long time, the HDP—the Kurdish national party and our former neighbours in Tarlabaşı—governed the 1.6 million population. However, they lost a recent election and now Erdoğan's AKP has the reins. I hoped by going there we'd better learn about the conflict, and how that conflict had created a Hemin.

We finished breakfast and walked back through the warrens of alleys to the dolmus station. Dolmuses are the ever-present, minibuses that ply this part of the country. A rusty blue minibus appeared. The driver opened the door by pulling on a long lever rigged from his seat.

Everyone seemed surprised to see us. I was enjoying being a novelty here because it was not a part of the world where novelty awakens in the locals a hope for economic opportunity, one that resulted in the always-unwelcome acts of pestering, persuading, and false promising.

Our dolmus drove not to Diyarbakır, but to a bakery. The driver got out and queued for bread.

"I like life here," I said to Evelyn wistfully. "In Germany, everything is so optimised it becomes rigid. Have you noticed how in Germany the sandwiches have either meat or cheese? Well, I once asked the woman if I could have one with meat *and* cheese."

"This was back before you were a vegetarian, then?"

"Why is your tongue poking out?" I asked. I had told Evelyn I was a vegetarian when we first met. Just another lie from the pile. One she'd uncover quickly when I absent-mindedly ordered crispy duck, my favourite food in the entire world.

"I still identify as a vegetarian," I said.

"And I identify as patient, but you should still get to the point."

"Anyway," I continued, "she said she couldn't do that because there isn't one with meat *and* cheese. So, then I said, can you take some cheese and put it in the one with meat, thus creating one with meat and cheese? She said no because there's no button on the till for meat *and* cheese."

"This is a great story," Evelyn said sarcastically. "I'm really on the edge of my seat."

"Thanks. I'm actually a professional storyteller." I looked down. "Or used to be. Anyway, then I said, 'Can I have it and you push whatever button you want? I can pay more. I WILL PAY MORE.' And I sort of flapped my wallet at her."

"What did she say?"

"She said I was holding up the line. Anyway, I left, stayed hungry, and thought warmly of England."

"Is it that different in England, then?" she asked.

"No, but in England, the people are really, really friendly while not giving you what you want. Customer service leaves a lot to be desired in your country."

"Leaves a lot to be desired," she repeated, licking her lips. "That has to be the most British sentence ever."

"What about *more tea, vicar*?"

"Sorry?" she asked, confused.

"Carry on ..."

"Leaves a lot to be desired," she said again, a pleased smile on her face. "Germans would just say it's shit. I'm learning a lot of strange English since we started dating. What was that word Nick said yesterday?"

"Goon?"

"Goon," she repeated. "I've never had a German boyfriend. Strange, right?"

"Really? Never?"

"Nope."

"Is there something wrong with German men?" I asked.

She made a clicking sound with her tongue as she considered it. "No, I just, well, I think it's easier for someone like me to date foreign men. That way, you can blame misunderstandings on the language or culture gap. Not actually, you know, on each other?"

"Interesting."

The driver got back with an enormous wagon wheel of bread. No one complained about the delay. He drove a bit more, then stopped because something was wrong with one of his tyres.

For five straight minutes, he kicked that tyre, the one directly beneath our seat, while I tried to think of a single thing about a tyre that kicking could improve, but I came up blank.

Again, no one complained, although I guess the tyre would have if it could. I looked around for Nick. The sexes sit apart on a dolmus—at least in this part of Turkey—which can often lead to Gender Jenga every time new people get on and seat shuffling must occur. They assumed Evelyn and I were married, so we could sit together. I craned my neck, looking for Nick and found him squashed in the back row and asleep already, a talent of his.

"People don't kick tyres in Germany," I said to underscore my point about how everything here was rich in nonchalant novelty.

She shifted in her seat. "I know what you mean," she said in a tone already hinting at a coming *but*. "But, I think maybe we like it because we know we don't really have to interact with it, because we have the money to avoid all its hard bits?"

"But I mean we're here on this dolmus, right? Watching a bread-rich man boot a tyre. We could be in the back of a taxi. Or driving our own car. Or riding a bike. Probably not riding a bike because it's like midday-on-Mars hot. Do you think the tyre has melted? Did I have a point?"

"I'm beginning to wonder."

"Anyway, I've made my point. I can't remember when or what it was, but I think you'll agree I have made it?"

She tapped her knee. "I think your point is that efficiency is the enemy of interesting?"

"Exactly!" I raised my head to the sky. "Exactly what I said. Or wanted to say. On the spectrum between order and chaos, Germany has swung too far towards order."

"I'll remind you of that when we have kids," she said, then rushed to correct herself. "*If.*"

"And I'll remind you of that when we need a permit to install a sunshade on our balcony to stop those kids from getting burnt."

Could I imagine us all in the years in the distant future? No, not really. But it was new that I was trying to.

Before her fertility news, accelerated timelines, and non-ultimatum ultimatums, I evaluated our relationship in small, discrete chunks—that was a great hour; what a fantastic night; something is a bit off today but I'm excited about the weekend.

Not anymore ...

Her revelations had blown out all our time horizons. I now had to imagine how anything that annoyed me about her—every trait, quirk, mannerism, weakness, strength—might morph and stretch and then break us over the two decades we'd need to bring a child to adulthood.

Because, as time goes on, the lens we view each other

through becomes nicked, scratched, and dirtied by the drudgery of our shared lives. I didn't even want to spend twenty years with myself, so how fair was it to ask someone else to?

We swapped to a different dolmus with more cooperative wheels. It took a while to arrive, but again, no one complained.

Hemin had arranged for us to stay with his best friends, a married couple called Karim and Yezda. "We'll spend an hour with them, then go out and explore," said Nick, as we disembarked our third dolmus, now on the outskirts of Diyarbakır.

"I'm not sure Diyarbakır works like that," Evelyn said as we retrieved our backpacks and found a small bit of space to sit, watching the minibuses pull in and out. "That you can just stroll around eating ice cream and buying souvenir mugs. Ugh, ants." She got back up. "At least not at the moment. Maybe I'm wrong. I'm not wrong."

Resting in the shade, we enjoyed the typical street life scenes of this part of the world: men, crouched on tiny plastic stools drinking even tinier teas; men, brows furrowed, staring down at chess games; men, huddled and loudly gesticulating and touching other men in acts of tight brotherhood; men, pulling and pushing piles of goods; men, convincing each other that the price of these goods could not be made cheaper for even their own mothers.

As we waited for Karim to arrive, Nick paced back and forth, his holdall slung over his shoulder, looking for rats to lead in song, as curious, bemused locals took turns peppering us with the same question: *why are you in Diyarbakır?*

We stood out here even more than in Mardin, and that was saying something.

A silver hatchback screeched to a stop in front of us, its driver's window down. "Evelyn? Adam?"

Karim was our age, solidly built, with thick black hair that curled at its edges, and a goatee flecked with silver touches. He jumped out and hugged us. "How was the drive?" he asked as he threw our rucksacks in the boot. I'd left my suitcase back in Istanbul, bringing only a modest seven shirts with me.

"Fine," Evelyn said. "The highway was empty."

His head jerked. "They took the highway? Usually they avoid it because there are too many bombings."

"Oh," Evelyn said. "We probably would have too if we'd known."

We set off. It was all of twenty seconds before the first checkpoint, which they waved us through, as Karim tapped out the beat of a Kurdish pop song, then cranked up through the gears, weaving and dodging through the traffic. I got the sense he knew every street and curve and pothole of his city. I checked twice that my seatbelt was on.

"It's actually a pretty good time to be here," he said enthusiastically. "Because of the referendum in Iraq, the HDP has an amnesty, so it's calmer than normal."

We zipped through another open checkpoint, manned by two bored armed soldiers on their phones. The city strongly reminded me of Hebron, a contested city on the border of Israel and Palestine, and one of the least-relaxing places I've ever been as a tourist. "Although there is a HDP rally later in the centre."

"Can we go?" Nick asked.

Karim made a sucking sound with his lips. "It's better *I* don't. I'm one of the few people here also active internationally. I'll get arrested again and have to spend ten days in prison, which is okay, but then I can't work, and I have much to do these days. You definitely can't go. They'll take you for journalists, which won't end well. Depending on how you feel about prison?"

"I'm not a big fan," said Evelyn as Karim veered sharply into the car park of a shopping mall.

"I'm also broadly anti-prison," I said. "All in all."

"I can't think of anything worse," said Nick. "Even death."

"Eh?" said Karim. "You get used to it." He parked. "Just nipping into Starbucks. Anyone want anything? The brownies are great."

"Nice guy," said Nick, turning so we could see him better as Karim disappeared for his coffee fix. "Bit intense."

"What do you make of the city so far?" Evelyn asked. "I'm confused."

"How is he finding his way?" said Nick. "It all looks the bloody same."

I nodded. "It's like all the buildings had a fight and dragged themselves away to be alone."

From what we'd seen so far, there were lots of new, five- and six-storey housing blocks dropped large distances from each other with little in-between. Each building had ground floor commercial spaces, almost all of which were vacant. There might be a small playground between them, but then no pavement connecting that to the buildings, so it would sit there unused, baking in the ferocious heat. It looked like it had been designed by a man in the sky.

Karim returned, visibly delighted with his two large bags of coffee. "There are few places here with anything good. Gotta stock up."

We rejoined the frenetic traffic.

"What's with the gaps?" I asked.

He chuckled, bullying his way between a truck and a motorbike. "Well, the idea is to get people to move into the buildings first. Then, they can fill the gaps later with shops and restaurants and stuff."

"Does that make sense to you?" Evelyn asked in a diplomatic tone.

"Wellllllll ..." He hesitated. "No? But not all that much here makes sense to me." He turned up the music I was secretly Shazaming.

"What's with all the Erdoğan pictures?" Nick asked, pointing at the enormous lampposts in the middle of the road, each of which had either an Erdoğan photo or the Turkish flag at its very top, perhaps seven metres from the ground.

Karim groaned. "Erdoğan came here last year for a speech. They put them along the whole route from the airport."

"Why are they still up?"

"No one dares to remove them," he said, disgust in his voice. "That shows the power he has now. If the HDP were in charge, they'd never have gone up."

A group of cars overtook us, pumping their horns. One had a pink ribbon stretched across its front.

"Wedding?" I asked.

"Yep," said Karim, giving three honks of his horn in solidarity. Along the edge of the road, and even in the centre of a roundabout, families picnicked. Were there even fewer parks here than Istanbul?

A few turns later, we reached the brand-new identikit building where Karim and his wife, Yezda, had recently moved. The four-storey complex didn't even have a paved road up to it yet, but that hadn't stopped them from starting the next block, diagonally opposite, across a patch of bare earth. I sheltered my eyes from the blinding sun.

"The old part is pretty," Karim said, reading my mind.

"And for much of the year, it's too hot to walk around, anyway."

"This is that part of the year, right?"

"Nah," he said with a chuckle.

I checked my phone—it was 40°C; a degree cooler than yesterday.

We found Yezda in the living room painting on an easel, a skinny black kitten circling her feet. Her delicate face was hidden behind a thick black curtain of hair, and heavy mascara. She seemed very at ease with herself and her situation, which we soon learned was nowhere near as harmonious as this living room scene suggested.

"The city feels kind of ... tense?" Nick said as we took seats on the many sofas. Karim and Yezda laughed. "Yes and no," Karim said. "It's tense for you. It's normal for us. Or normal tense anyway."

"Blimey," said Nick.

"Yeah, we've had better years," Karim lamented. "A lot changed here in 2015, after the national elections. HDP got 13 per cent of vote and Erdoğan only got 40 per cent, so couldn't make his majority government. He retaliated, as he likes to do. My boss was imprisoned and I lost my job."

"I'm sorry," Evelyn said.

Yezda understood us when we spoke, but was too shy to reply in English, so Karim played interpreter. He turned to her, inviting her into the conversation. "And Yezda's cousin is in prison, as you probably know?" he said.

Nick and I swapped blank looks. "He's Selahattin Demirtaş, the Kurdish Obama," said Evelyn. "I met him once in Berlin. Briefly."

"There's a Kurdish Obama?" I asked. "No one told me."

Apparently, this was funny.

"That was a nickname in the press," Yezda said, via Karim. "He's the leader of the HDP," Karim clarified, pouring out some more tea for us. "A pretty popular guy, but popularity is not really a currency Kurds can profit from. He's been in prison in the mountains for the past few months, swept up in one of Erdoğan's many purges." Karim looked off at what I assumed was the direction of those mountains.

"What do you do to relax?" I asked, hoping we could do it too, and then we'd all be, well, relaxed? Karim and Yezda were perfectly hospitable and made a lovely first impression, but everything around them seemed oppressive. It was like being hosted by the captain of the *Titanic*, telling you about the good times when there were still lifeboats.

"We don't relax," Yezda said, and Karim translated. "So many of our friends are in prison that if we do anything to switch off, anything that doesn't help them, we just feel guilty."

Karim took back over. "If we go to Starbucks, plain-clothed police listen from three tables over. It just makes you uncomfortable. Social life we do privately."

"I think I'd go crazy," said Evelyn.

Karim grinned. "We have, probably. But you can't escape it." He looked out the window to that nearby building site, at the under-construction housing block where two men shovelled cement. "If the government is angry at the Kurds, and they're angry right now, they'll slow that project down, hold back those men's pay. Everything is politics here."

So that was where Hemin got it from—the one-track political mind looping a song of revolution.

"How come your English is so flawless?" Nick asked.

A sly smile escaped Karim's lips, one of the first, soon chased away by embarrassment. "I did a PhD in the USA."

"What was the topic?"

"Conflict resolution."

We laughed. "A job for life here."

An hour later, we parked and climbed up some steps to the top of the enormous black, five-metre high, basalt city walls. We looked down at the rubble of recently cleared land. This city was famous for this wall, the second longest in the world. The first sections of which were built in 297 AD.

Karim checked a fact with Yezda. "Fifty thousand people used to live within these," he said. "Twenty-three thousand people have been displaced." He took a deep breath. "They're punishing us for the war. For daring to fight back."

We looked down at a small slum erected in one of the cleared patches of land. Several homes had tarpaulin for roofs and an impromptu football game was taking place, using a segment of brick for goal posts. Near it, gangly, gender-divided teenagers stood shyly in bodies that didn't quite fit yet, making flirtatious side-eye at each other.

"The wall's a funny story actually," said Karim. "Well, more funny-sad, but that's all stories here." He checked another fact with Yezda. "So, there was a governor appointed here from Ankara, but he found the city too hot, so he started removing the wall so the air could better circulate." He hung his head as he spoke, embarrassed on the man's behalf. "There was no logic to this, of course. That's not how air works. Anyway, he kept dismantling the wall until a French architect made a lot of noise about it in Europe. These walls are over two thousand years old."

"What are they doing with the space they're clearing?" Evelyn asked.

"What they always do," he said dejectedly.

"Shopping malls?" she guessed.

He laughed. "Some of those, yes. Otherwise, they just build big houses for rich people. There were over one hundred historical buildings here: churches, synagogues, etc. going right back to pagan times, but the government is destroying it brick by brick."

Yezda stroked his arm, trying to gee him back up, and we climbed down off the wall and walked the city's main shopping street—long and straight and dotted with police barricades. It was quiet, many of the shops shuttered.

The idea this was a place you would come—rather than try desperately to flee—seemed ludicrous. From behind the stacked sandbags, the eyes of the police and army watched as we moved. In the middle of the road, street crews were ripping up the cobblestones and replacing them with asphalt. "The Turkish government is paranoid about cobblestones, because people used them as barricades, or throw them at police," Yezda explained.

"This is the former cultural centre," Karim said, next to a boarded-up brick building. "It's closed."

"It's heavy, this tour," said Nick.

"Yes," he said. "It is. Let's eat ..."

In a roadside restaurant, on a new block so finished it had pavements, lighting, plants, and a shaded walkway, Karim raised his glass of fizzing coke. "We're celebrating," he said, beginning a toast of our non-alcoholic drinks. "They published Yezda's brother's book today."

"What kind of book?" I asked, happy to be on a topic I knew more about.

"A collection of short stories he wrote in prison."

"Do you think it will help get him out?" Evelyn asked.

Yezda shook her head. "No. But it might stop him from being forgotten."

"Did you expect him to be imprisoned as he got more popular?" Evelyn asked.

"We thought he was too popular to be arrested," Karim said. "The backlash was strong but not strong enough. The worst thing you can be in prison is forgotten. That's why the book is so important."

"Do you think there's any chance to get Erdoğan booted out of office, or is he too powerful now?" Nick asked. Karim discussed it with Yezda. I noticed the worry lines under their eyes now. How all this had left them prematurely aged, as it had Hemin.

"There is always a chance," Karim said. "They've imprisoned most of the educated people and replaced them with ultra-nationalists. I don't think the new people can keep the country running properly. If you lose the economy, you lose the country."

"Is the entire city dry?" Nick asked, looking disappointingly at the dregs of his pomegranate juice.

"Yes ..." Karim winked. "Unless you know where to look."

"Are Kurds big drinkers, or is it just Hemin?" Evelyn asked. Cheer erupted from people at a long table in the corner who were celebrating another wedding. "He can drink for several of us, that's true," said Karim mischievously. "We're a conservative culture, but mostly a secular one. We drink. Erdoğan is trying to create a new Muslim narrative, mostly through misappropriating events from the past. It's a problem for liberal Turks as well, of course."

Back in the car, driving out of the city, we passed several covered markets and bazaars. You could feel there was a traditional way of life here—slow and unrushed and even romantic, with people lingering to sit, talk, trade, and relax out on the street—that people were trying to keep against significant opposition. That, like Mardin, this would be a big, open museum, only unlike Mardin, Diyarbakır—because of its location and the ethnicity of its population—was too important in the present. And so, the worst of modernity—soldiers and their guns and their nationalism, with their enormous Turkish flags and pictures of a vainglorious Erdoğan strapped to the top of every lamppost—were here, blighting it.

It grew dark. We drove into the woods, parking at the edge of a bar, a place with no sign, hidden deep amongst lights strung up between trees.

"Now, to a proper toast," said Nick, raising his beer bottle. "Thanks for today. You've been great hosts." Nick looked relaxed for perhaps the first time on this trip. We were a long, long way from nappy changes and peekaboo. We clinked glasses and bottles.

"Where did you meet Hemin?" Evelyn asked. They turned to each other and grinned. With this simple question, they transformed: the bags under their eyes emptied, the years fell from their shoulders, and the worry lines on their foreheads relaxed. They were no longer here, with us, hiding in the woods, thinking of friends killed or imprisoned. Instead, they were back in their youth—the three of them, young communists drinking soapy beer in a loud dive bar, the walls covered with graffiti, discussing Marx and the revolution they were sure was just over there, ripe for the taking.

"Did you know that Hemin comes from a very prominent family?" Karim asked as the spell wore off. Hemin had talked about his village, how he hoped to return there and work the land once again, but not much about his upbringing.

"Yes," Karim continued, "his grandfather was a famous imam. A brilliant poet, really, a true intellectual." He grasped Yezda's hand. There'd been almost no moment since we'd arrived when he and Yezda weren't touching. Their delight with each other was in every glance, touch, whispered word, arm stroke, and handhold. I didn't envy their life here but saw that when the future feels far away, and out of your control, it's easier to appreciate what's good in the present.

They were good for each other. "Hemin really never mentioned his grandfather?" Karim asked.

We shook our heads.

He frowned. "It's a sad story."

"Oh, not another one?" Nick joked at what was becoming the catchphrase of this trip. Karim sighed deeply. "In the 90s, the state burnt down his family's home. They lost everything and had to move to Istanbul. Hemin worked throughout his childhood. He sold matches on the street."

Suddenly so many more things about Hemin made sense: the sadness he fought hard to keep at bay but was always there, simmering just below his surface, visible in how much he drank, how late he rose, and in the pragmatic violence of his ideology. His beliefs made more sense too. Someone who had to work throughout their childhood would be drawn to communism, in which resources are shared equally (in theory).

Spending time with Karim and Yezda also helped me understand the magnitude of his move to Berlin. Before it, Hemin was probably like them: living here but unable to relax, every minute not working on the cause, a minute wasted. Now he had freedom, but it had cost him dearly. How much guilt must he feel about the people he left behind?

Back at the flat, we bedded down for the night, draping ourselves across the apartment's various couches. I slept poorly, and in the early morning, wandered out to the bathroom. The kitchen light was on, and I poked my head round the door. Karim was sitting in a cloud of his own cigarette smoke. He looked lost, the skin under his eyes dry and irritated.

"Why are you still up?" I asked.

"Can't sleep," he mumbled.

"You have that problem a lot?"

He raised his hand from the keyboard, then let it drop. "I usually just work. Are you going to write about us, Adam? Hemin said you're a travel writer. Is that why you're here?"

"About the Kurds? No."

"Why not?" he asked. "We need the help."

"I'm not a serious writer. Evelyn is the political one. I'm more of a ..." I thought back to my bread and cheese story on the dolmus. "I don't really know what I am."

"There are enough serious writers."

"It won't help," I said. "I don't have many readers."

"It always helps," he said ominously.

"Don't work too hard, okay?" I said and left, knowing he would because Yezda's brother was languishing in prison. Of course, they would keep working, fighting, and losing. Because the fight wasn't fair. Which didn't mean they should stop. Nor that they should continue. If you only have bad options, you're damned either way.

Tourism will return to Diyarbakır when relations between the Turks and Kurds improve. There's too much history and specialness for it not to. In the meantime, no one is waiting. The Kurds are getting on with their lives. Making them the best they can be. And that's what I would take from it. Seeing those wedding parties, flirting teenagers, old couples sitting silently on benches, families crammed together on the verges of busy roads sharing meals, and the sly touches between Karim and Yezda made me happy.

Gave me hope.

In every place in the world, no matter how forsaken, repressed, oppressed, inhospitable or uninhabitable, eyes are meeting and shy smiles are becoming hands that touch briefly behind backs or feet that stroke under tables.

Coupling. Love. People checking their egos, ignoring their doubts, silencing their inner critics, summoning their best selves, ironing borrowed shirts, putting on their rosiest glasses, suspending their disbelief, laughing in the face of the odds, deciding this time it will be different as they get back on the roller coaster for the greatest, most exalting, humbling human experience: one that somehow, despite its prevalence, its disgustingly everyday pedestrian common-ness, refuses to become banal.

Evelyn was asleep when I returned to the living room. I slipped onto her couch and wrapped myself around her and that was how we slept until we awoke to the cat nuzzling us, letting us know it was time to move on to Van, where I hoped the stories would be less sad.

18

Van was a relaxed tourist town near the Iranian border, famous for cats with differently coloured eyes. After Diyarbakır, it was a shock to be in a normal city, one with no police checkpoints, sandbags, and improvised high-street barricades.

The city was at war, however, but a war against baldness, wonky teeth, protruding foreheads, and upturned noses. A war fought with the scalpel—its street full of the bandaged and surgically wounded, clutching plastic shopping bags full of designer clothes for the new them.

It was our last stop with Nick. He'd always planned to spend just a part of his trip with us, then the rest on his own. How much of each he'd never revealed until today. He claimed he wanted to head up to Giresun to do some sailing, but I wondered if we'd done something wrong?

Evelyn wasn't feeling well, so only he and I went out for his last night. The first bar rejected us because we were men alone. The second barman looked unsure, checked with a colleague, then brought us to a corner table, checking first that there were no women around.

"You stay here," he said as we sat down.

"Jesus," said Nick as the man walked back to the bar to get our beers. "Bit over the top, isn't it? Like we're some kind of predator."

"Perhaps they have a problem with harassment here?"

"Maybe."

"So, good trip?" I said. "Get what you wanted?"

He stared at the wall behind me. "Sleep was what I wanted. And to see Mardin and Diyarbakır." He fumbled a cigarette from the pack. "So yeah, I guess so? The day with Karim and Yezda was terrific. I feel like I get it more now, don't you? The Kurd thing."

I nodded. "How did you find travelling with Evelyn? She's entertaining, right?" I wanted someone to validate what I was seeing, which was her overwhelming, albeit complicated, awesomeness.

He looked up. "Is she afraid of silence?"

I chuckled. "Seems that way, yeah."

"She has very strong opinions. I mean, compared to Antje."

"You prefer your women to shut up and make the casserole?"

"No. It's ..." he searched for the right words. "Not an insult."

"You remember how I described her to you after I met her in that bar?"

He pulled out a cigarette and tapped it against the pack. "It was soooo ridiculous."

I waited for him to say it. He frowned. "Okay, I have forgotten. But it was ridiculous. I stand by that part."

"I said she was mother-of-my-children-great."

"You did too," he said, snorting. "So, she's pregnant?"

"No. But her cards are very on the table."

"Show me a thirty-four-year-old woman whose cards are not on the table?"

"But it's, well, a lot? Right?" I was a stuck record.

He lit his cigarette. "What about it is a lot?"

"To get to decide that? Whether a human should come into existence? Like an actual real-life human person with like earlobes and elbows and stuff?"

"I know how humans look," he said, taking his first long puff.

"And while Evelyn's really wonderful, she has some annoying traits."

"Uh-huh."

"It's like, well, her handbag, right?"

His eyes narrowed. "We're going to spend my last night talking about her handbag?"

"Sure, it sounds trivial but, I mean, I'll set the scene for you." I moved my hands apart like the opening of a stage's curtain. "Her and I have come out the subway and we're walking down her street. We're approaching her building's big, grey door, right?"

"Fascinating stuff, this."

"We've reached the door now, Nick. Guess what happens?"

He blew out a cloud of smoke. "Er, you go in?"

"If only we went in." My voice rose with indignation. "If only. What actually happens is she stops and seems confused there's a door there. As if there wasn't before. Then she remembers she needs her key. She opens her incredibly messy, system-less bag and starts rooting around. And, of course, she can't find it."

"Tragic," he said.

"And so, we stand there like bloody idiots as she raises the bottom of her bag up and makes that *grrr* noise she always makes and, it just, well, it drives me crazy."

"I see that," he says, but he was looking away now, over towards the pool tables.

"And if it's driving me crazy now, how crazy will it drive me in, I don't know, seven years?"

He glanced back at me, his voice emotionless. "Do you think you don't have any annoying traits?"

"It's not even really about the bag thing, you know," I said, feigning nonchalance. "Let's say I get over it, the whole bag-door-key problem, and we have a kid. A daughter. With Evelyn's wild blonde hair. Glorious little thing she is. Little scamp. When I look at her, am I going to be secretly thinking, *you so almost didn't exist*? If your mum had just been like 2 per cent more disorganised, or I was 2 per cent more scared, NO YOU." I took a deep breath. "And, yeah, that's a lot, you know?"

He blew out a ring of smoke. "You're a lot, doofus."

"I'm pouring my heart out here and all you can say in support is, *you're a lot, doofus*?"

He stubbed out the nub of his cigarette into the ashtray and leaned forward, pointing his index finger at my face. "Do you think, when Evelyn was younger, reading trashy Mills and Boon romance books or whatever they had in Germany, daydreaming about the man she'd have children with, build a sodding family with. Do you think she imagined that," he lunged round the edge of the table and yanked at the blue cord attached to my belt loop, "he'd wear a fucking key-cord chain on his pants EVERY SINGLE DAY? DO YOU KNOW HOW INCREDIBLY DORKY THIS THING IS?"

He dropped it and it swung free, down near the floor. He sat back down.

"It's dorky?" I asked quietly, lifting the cord and keys it expertly secured back up and into my pocket. "But we never stand at my front door like idiots though, do we?"

He flapped a hand at me dismissively. He fumbled at the pack, and I assumed he was going to light a second cigarette, but he tapped the pack's edge against the table, then put it down on its side. "You're in it," he said. "You and Evelyn, for better or worse. You're on the tracks and there's no reverse. And once the kid is here, once you're in the parenting trenches, you don't have time for this intellectual ..." he paused. "Wankery."

"Wankery?"

He doubled down. "Wankery. And anyway, doofus, what's the alternative?"

"To what?"

"To giving it a proper go."

I shrugged. "Not giving it a proper go?"

He pointed his finger at me. "The alternative's shit, pal. It's finding a new woman and repeating the first six months forever. Then when it gets hard, or loses its sparkle, you quit and find a new one. I've done it. But the more often you do it, the less novelty there is in it, too." He took a swig of beer, then burped. "Before long, you catch yourself telling the same stories, the same half lies, using the wrong name for them in bed."

I chuckled, trying to remember if I'd ever done that. "Then," he continued, enjoying the raptness of my attention, "you notice that, when you're introducing her to your mates, they don't even bother to learn her name or ask her questions because they know she won't be sticking around."

"Bleak," I said, about this imagined future.

He nodded. "T'is, yeah."

"But how do you know you found the right person, then? To end that cycle with?"

He blew a raspberry. "You're never going to know, are you? And maybe it is the right person and then they die young anyway, like with my dad. Or maybe they're wrong, but you stay together regardless, because you love your kids and that's what's best for them, like almost everyone?"

"But I mean, you've turned things around, no? Beaten your demons."

A quiet laugh became a howl. "You don't beat your demons. You just quieten them for a time."

"That's ..." I slapped my cheeks, "incredibly depressing."

We broke the rules and moved over to play some pool. "You hanging around Van for a few more days?" he asked as I failed miserably to pot a simple black ball to the corner pocket.

I shrugged. "I think so. Then we'll do some nature stuff. Evelyn likes nature. I might have told her I like it too, can't remember."

Over the next hour, we somehow controlled our desire to hit on the bar's dozen women, playing pool as Nick bested me effortlessly. I pretended I was letting him win because it was his last night. He pretended to believe me. They were lies, but good lies.

He stopped as he walked back to the hotel. A street light bathed him in yellow light. "I will say one thing and it's not advice and you shouldn't base any decisions on it. But something is more likely to work when it has to."

19

"Did I tell you about the time I got lost in the Rwandan jungle?" she asked after she'd fidgeted through an oppressive (for her) three-minute-long silence. We were sitting in our sixth dolmus of the day, travelling north to visit a lake Karim and Yezda had recommended.

"Five times, at least. It's a good one. I'll never go into the jungle again. Not that I really have much until now."

"Oh, right," she said, disappointed. "Well, did I tell you about the disastrous date I went on where the guy streaked me?"

"Yeah, really weird."

She lowered her head; you could almost hear the cogs turning. "You tell me a story, then?" she suggested when those clogs jammed.

"I wouldn't mind listening to some music."

"We can talk," she said defensively. "We still have stuff to talk about."

"Sure, but we don't have to."

She looked around.

She tapped her chin.

She looked around. "If you could be ... any celebrity in the world, what celebrity would you be?"

I groaned.

She groaned. "Don't even answer," she said and patted me on the arm. "Listen to your music."

"Why are you so scared of silence?" I asked.

"Scared is not the right word." The dolmus driver honked the horn as we narrowly missed an oncoming lorry while overtaking another lorry.

"What is the right word?" I asked.

Her nose wrinkled. "Apprehensive, maybe? Why aren't you scared? Wouldn't it mean we're out of the beginning?"

"Not all silences are the same. It's a good sign when you feel comfortable enough with someone that you can just be."

"Maybe," she conceded.

"Could it be that you're scared that I'm going to read too much into a silence?"

"Hmm, I don't know? I just ... What does it mean, the silence?" she asked.

"It means we've spent an extraordinary amount of time together since we came to Turkey. And even more in the last week." I lifted her hand and kissed it. As much public affection as I'd risk in this part of the country, which was not as liberal as Istanbul. "Everything's fine. Relax."

"I'll try," she said. "I guess I've never really reached the point where you run out of things to say."

"Then we achieved something! Congrats."

"Uh-huh."

"It's temporary," I reassured.

"Okay." Eventually, some ten hours after we started, we arrived in the nearest town to this ominous lake. "How far away is the lake?"

"Not far, I don't think," I said with feigned confidence.

I'd agreed to look after this part of the trip as she'd handled the logistics of Mardin, Diyarbakır, and Van, or what Nick had let her handle anyway. We were in the town of Aralık, the nearest to the lake. I slung my backpack up onto my shoulder. "We can walk."

"Did you actually check, though?" she asked, her hand hovering over her bag but not picking it up.

"Yessss," I said. "I think it's like an hour, maybe? But a pleasant walk. Probably."

She got out her phone. "It's nine hours!"

I put my rucksack down. "*Oh?* It looked close on the map."

"Are you taking the Nick role in this trip? I thought you researched all this?"

I did, of course, but Adam-style, which is casual and assumes the universe exists only to grant my every whim and desire.

"We could take another dolmuş?" I suggested.

She frowned. "I'm not sure enough people go to this lake that it'll be on a dolmuş route."

We asked around for a dolmuş. Regrettably, she was right. The lake, which we knew as Black Lake, was not the tourist draw we had hoped.

"Travelling is different as a woman," Evelyn said as we left the dolmuş station, walking the direction where someone had said there might be a taxi. "You're a bit more careful what you walk into."

"Are all women like that, though?" I asked.

She stopped to put her hair up in a ponytail. It was frightfully hot, the heat an ever-present menace on this trip. "I assume so, yeah?" she said. "It's like, the other day in Van, when you were off with Nick visiting cats. I felt better and so went to the mall because I need shoes. This guy approached me and kept asking where I was from. I said Germany, but he kept asking me if I was Russian."

"Why Russian?"

"They use it here as a synonym for prostitute, or so I've read. Anyway, he kept following me and so eventually I had to go into a clothes shop and hide in the changing rooms until he went away."

"Really? That's horrible."

"I mean, I didn't even tell you until now, so it can't have been a big deal. But it kind of is, isn't it?" She squinted. "It just reminded me of what it's like to travel alone as a woman. At least in certain parts of the world."

There was no taxi where they had said. "We could hitchhike?"

"I read about hitchhiking here before we came." She frowned. "Because I do my research. Because I have to."

"And what did it say?"

"It said it's fine."

I clicked my fingers. "Boom."

"Yeah, but then the article started listing all the precautions you should take, and it kept going and going and going. I almost got a repetitive strain injury scrolling to the bottom."

"What were they? The precautions."

"Don't get into a car with more than one person. Don't tell them you're Russian, have ever been to Russia, or know anyone who has been to Russia. Don't look them in the eye. Don't sit in the front.

"We can pretend to be married. Everyone thinks we are anyway."

She wagged her finger. "No, they know that trick, apparently. If we're married, that only proves we're having sex, which means I'm no longer a virgin, which means I'm fair game."

"Seriously?"

"The suggestion was to say you're my uncle. That way you're responsible for me and they know you will protect me, but I could also still be a virgin, which means something around here, apparently."

"I'm not sure I look old enough to be your uncle."

I expected her to confirm this. No confirmation was forthcoming.

Ten minutes later, on the far side of town, we finally found a taxi, communicated with its driver via Google Translate, and were on our way to the lake. Or an area near it he said had a pension we could stay in for the night. It was uphill all the way. The driver stopped outside a pension, a handsome property lined with multicoloured wooden fence posts, behind which a tall, glass-fronted restaurant stood overlooking a wild stream.

We were two steps from the taxi when a rake-thin man opened its equally colourful gate, grinning and waving enthusiastically, beckoning us inside.

"He's keen," I said.

"Looks nice," said Evelyn. He bowed his head as we passed, as if we were long-awaited, honoured guests. He talked fast and moved fast and had scruffy, spiky black hair, only a few remaining teeth, and a manic edge. When it was clear we couldn't communicate, no matter how hard and fast he tried, he got out his phone, made a call, and handed it to me.

"Hello," said a young, male, somewhat distant voice.

"Hi."

"Welcome, friend. You need room?"

"Yes," I confirmed.

"It's eighty lira, including breakfast, twenty-five more if you want dinner. Father show you?"

I repeated this to Evelyn, swapping to German for

privacy. She took a last look around and then nodded in what I took as broad agreement of the terms. I covered the speaker with my hand. "Does it seem like anyone else is here, though?"

"Does that matter?" she asked.

"It's just nice if there's other people around to hang out with. It's not like we can talk to this guy."

She shrugged. "We won't be here long and we've no idea how far away the next pension is. We might walk all day and not find something. Not that there's all that much day left."

I removed my hand. "Okay," I said to the discombobulated voice. "One night for now."

"Great. That's just great. Please return the phone to Father."

Father went to the nearest door, which led into a lounge/restaurant, beautifully lit in the afternoon light. It was completely empty, and dust swirled in the air. He lowered the handle; the door was locked. A wave of panic flashed across his gaunt face. He was little more than cheek bones with eyes. He swirled on the spot, then ducked down and began searching the floor, running his hands through the tall blades of grass.

No key.

He started furiously lifting stones. Then he was upright again, his enormous eyes darting around in an unfocused frenzy as he put the phone back to his ear and gave his son hell, or so it sounded.

"I'm not getting a good feeling," I said in German.

"What's the matter?"

A minute passed as I chewed my lip, watching Father shout at his progeny and hunt around in his overgrown garden.

I took a step back and subtly waved at Evelyn to follow me. "Vibe check?" I said, then regretted.

"What are you, fifteen?"

"VIBE CHECK," I repeated.

"Fine," she said. "I'm fine. Good vibes."

"Doesn't he seem a bit murderous?"

"He's just very thin."

"And frantic?"

"He's lost the key. Give him a minute. I'm sure he's a very nice man."

"A very frantic, murderous, nice man?"

The man lowered the phone, tilted his head, and gave what was supposed to be a reassuring, open-mouth smile, but, if you swapped the phone for a knife, was actually a perfect horror-slasher movie poster.

I gave him a thumbs up; it was best to stay on his good side. Was this his good side? I hoped this wasn't his good side.

He shouted some more into the phone and continued searching. Another minute passed. "I feel like a Christmas miracle," I whispered. "Like he was minutes away from being declared bankrupt, and then we've arrived."

Evelyn crossed her arms. "I think that's pretty accurate, yeah."

"I don't like the feeling."

"He'll find the key. We'll get a room. *Fine. All fine.*"

"How do you lose the key to your own hostel and/or restaurant?" I asked.

"Who says and/or?"

I sighed. "It's the stress."

"What stress? You are the stress."

"It's just not a sign of a thriving enterprise, is all. Or a well-run enterprise. He's inefficient. He's incompetent."

"He's lost his key," she said matter-of-factly.

"He should have a keychain," I said, tugging on mine. My keys sprang forth, ready for use, and as they did, they jangled. The man stopped his sweep of a nearby mostly dirt flowerbed to look up expectantly, like a dog who has smelt bacon. Seeing they were my keys, his face cracked into a thousand tiny pieces of sharp despair.

I put my keys away. It took neither time nor effort.

"So nerdy," she said. "Stupid keychain."

"You been talking to Nick about my keychain?"

"Why would I talk to Nick about your keychain? Don't you think we've better things to talk about?"

I edged closer to the backpacks we'd left at the top of the garden steps. The man saw this and stood up, shouting some more in the phone, tugging on unkempt strands of his wild hair. He moved to search nearer the gate. I gave Evelyn some vicious evil-eye, sliding another step away. There was a small metal bin near my right foot. I lifted it up: a silver key lay there.

I checked to see if the man had noticed. He had not.

I checked the see if Evelyn had noticed. She had not.

I carefully put the metal bin back down, turned, and scooped up my backpack. "What are you doing?" Evelyn asked with alarm. I pointed at my invisible watch. "I'm done. This guy is annoying me."

I opened the small but cheerfully coloured gate and stepped back down to the narrow road, assuming Evelyn would follow me, because it would be too awkward not to. I glanced back, and yes, she was picking up her bag. Father, sensing that his miracle was bolting, dropped the phone in panic.

She followed me out. I sped down the path, striding away from this man and his desperation. His eyes, previously wide, were now 90 per cent of his head. He scooped up the phone and ran after us, waving it with one hand above his head and shrieking. He passed Evelyn, then me, turning and facing me, walking backwards, trying to block my path.

I refused to take the phone he was shaking in my face like a maraca. He kept pace with me, holding the phone next to my ear. "Please wait," said Son. "I am there in fifteen minutes, okay?"

I stopped and took the phone. "We're going to look at what else is around," I said. "Thanks anyway. But no."

I gave the phone back, and we hurried on before Son could answer. Father followed us for a time, ranting into his phone and ranting at us. Evelyn said nothing, just kept her head down, trailing a metre or two behind me, her face patchy and red, her eyes skittish. A minute or two later, we turned a corner, and I glanced back. The man had stopped.

I let Evelyn catch up. "What was that?" she said, pushing me in the chest.

"Went well, I thought?"

"Why didn't we just wait?" She glanced back. "That poor, nice man."

"You found him *nice*?"

She pulled out her bottle of water. "You made a horrible scene over nothing."

"He didn't speak English, or know where the key to his own hotel was? Then he made us wait for ages. And he seemed totally desperate. It was icky. All of it. Just icky."

She pointed up at my face. "*You* made it icky. I don't know what came over you. That was just weird. Are you secretly weird? Have you hidden that weirdness until now?"

I tried to work out why I'd reacted so strongly. My behaviour had resulted in a certain palpable ickiness. I had also, perhaps, broken a lightly skeletal, destitute man's heart while putting Evelyn through the sort of awkward scene she detests. She likes to help people. We could have helped him. I ruined that, and now we were lost, with nowhere to stay.

I held my hand out towards her water. "Get your own water," she said, pulling it away.

A flash, black 4x4 pulled up. Its window descended electronically. "Hello," said its driver. I recognised his voice. It was Son.

"Hi," I said, leaning down to the height of the window.

"We talked on the phone," he said.

"Uh-huh."

"I am here now." This seemed obvious. "If you want, you get in and we go to the pension?"

I looked up and down the road. We'd not passed a single building since we left the pension. I tried to read Evelyn's face, but she was keeping it deliberately, stubbornly blank. The idea that we must not only see the old man again but spend one or perhaps multiple days alone with him, in his abandoned, poorly run, objectively attractive, multicolour-posted pension didn't fill me with excitement.

Mostly, in fact, it filled me with embarrassment and a smidgen of terror. It's okay to make a mistake—and storming off like that was probably a mistake—but why return to that mistake and sit in it for several excruciating days?

"No," I said. "That's okay. *Thanks.*"

Son, sitting in the driver's seat, broke eye contact and looked out through the windscreen where he took a long, melancholic breath before returning his eyes to me for a last assault on my conscience. "I'm sorry that it took so long, okay? But it's no problem now. We have the key. Everything is fine."

"It's fine," said Evelyn in German.

"Is it though?" I said to her. "I just don't think I can look him in the face again. It's going to be so awkward."

"*You* made it awkward."

I scraped my teeth across my bottom lip. "Sorry," I said to Son. "But we're going to look around. It's a nice day. A pleasant hike. Maybe we will come back later?"

He blinked slowly. "Okay."

He turned on the engine and drove away. "Well," said Evelyn. "You broke his son's heart now as well. Maybe you want them to call his mother down here so you can insult her?"

"She's buried in the garden."

Evelyn tried hard not to laugh. She failed and soon we were both giggling. "I found the key," I said, because the truth was important to her and that made it important to me.

If I thought she was angry before, she was furious now, teeth gritted, steam coming from her ears. I took a few steps away in case she spontaneously combusted.

"It was under the small metal bin," I said.

"When did you find it?" She stamped her foot. "I can't believe this."

"Just before we left. *I* left."

"Why didn't you say something? We could have avoided all of this?"

"I had already decided I wanted to leave."

"Why didn't you discuss that with me?" She picked up her bag. "We're supposed to be a team. Aren't you supposed to be good at this? At being part of a team. I don't understand you."

She stomped off.

"Don't stomp off. I hate it when you stomp off when we argue."

She considered stopping, then carried on. "Well, you can just do whatever you want, so why can't I walk off?"

I ran after her and pulled the backpack off her shoulder

to stop her. "I think," I said with a sigh. I pointed. "Sit with me on this log thing." Reluctantly, she agreed. "I have some issues about control," I began. I took off my hat and wiped away the sweat on my head. "Or rather, feeling that I've lost control. It's maybe why Nick and I are friends. I remember something I read, it was a study of people who moved abroad as adults. Looking at their like motivations and stuff. Do you know what most of them had in common?"

She considered it because she enjoyed knowing stuff, figuring things out, and she was good at it. "A dislike of their own culture?" she guessed.

"No. Although that probably helps."

"A love of travel?"

"Good guesses, but no. It's an overbearing mother."

She laughed. "That can't be true."

"Nick's mother is overbearing. So was mine. I think that's why I have some issues around control. Around obligation."

"That explains a lot," she said. "Or at least the last few weeks."

"Hey, come on, I haven't bolted from you. I'm here, I'm trying." I hugged her. She let me, just about. "There was just something about how he was acting," I continued. "About how much he obviously needed us. Or our money. It just seemed like I had no choice. Like we were obligated by his need. I found it just a real turn-off."

"Okay," she said. "I suppose. We all have our things. Mine is more about the truth and trust and stuff. But okay. I'll try to understand."

We continued on down the road. Walking helped. It was difficult to stay mad at myself because, all around us, nature was putting on a hell of a show. The road continued to curve upwards, bringing us ever closer to the low, wispy clouds. We were walking near that gorgeous stream as dragonflies swooped and bees frolicked, sexing up flowers, while ants marched and crappy caterpillars became magnificent butterflies. A cow passed us, ringing the bell around its neck with each hoofed step.

Five minutes later, a haggard lady appeared, stopping us to repeat a word while flapping her arms around. "I know that word," Evelyn said like a detective handed a vital clue. A few seconds passed as the woman said the word four more times.

"Cow!" Evelyn said triumphantly, with a fist pump. "It means cow! She wants to know if we've seen her cow? Yes." Evelyn said in baby Turkish and pointing back the way we'd come. "Cow. *Yes*. Go. That way."

It was a spectacular walk. I started, perhaps naively, to believe all this beauty could heal the day, assuming somewhere over yonder there was a pension we'd reached before we expired from thirst, hunger, coldness, sadness, or bickering.

"It's one of my biggest fears, actually," I said. "That I'd be an overbearing dad."

"Huh," she said. "We've never talked about the kind of parents we'd want to be. I heard this theory that there is a parent for every age. So, some like the babies, some toddlers, some teens."

"Teens," I said, anticipating her next question. "I'm sure I'll enjoy parenting teens best. I wasn't very good at being a child. I just wanted to be an adult, so I could be free."

"Of your mother? She can't have been that overbearing?"

"My mum's parents were abusive. Or at least, neglectful to the point of abuse. We were her chance to do things differently. To create the family she would have wanted. Her and my dad smothered us with kindness. Which is the best way to be smothered, I guess, other than maybe in peanut butter. I didn't answer your question. What was your question?"

"What kind of parent do you want to be?"

"Right." I nodded. "*Right*. Well, what I'm saying is that they focused on making us happy at all times, not on making us competent, functional humans. Maybe that's why I'm so bad at everyday human things like spinach and spark plugs. And it's why I have a problem with control. They never really wanted us to grow up or become independent because they were getting so much validation and love from us children. Anyway, this is a long rambling speech and what I want to say is that I think a parent's job is to make themselves obsolete."

"Perfect," she said, smiling. "That's how I see it, too. That was my parents' model. Montessori, basically. They actually pushed us out of the nest when we were nineteen. It was traumatic at the time, but the right decision."

"What didn't they do well?" I asked.

"Emotions. Feelings. Conflict. That is why I suck at it. Why I run away sometimes. I think, for a lot of years, they didn't really like each other. We got caught in the middle. They also put us in boxes at a young age. I was the brainy one and my sister was the funny one. And once you're in that box, a lot of your identity gets associated with that thing. You get trapped by your talents."

"That's a nice phrase," I said.

"It took me a long time to figure that out. And a lot of self-help books. Rather than just throwing myself into social situations, like my sister did, I treated people as an academic subject, like how I studied the solar system or something. But that's not how people work. They aren't rational," she said, pointing at me, "as you've just shown back there. Humans are weird."

"We are," I said and followed it up with "Eureka,"

because I'd just seen a sign nailed to a tree: *pension*. It was pointing towards a large, dilapidated, barn-like building further upstream.

It, too, had a fence made of small posts; none painted bright colours.

They showed us to a small, dark upstairs room of so much wood I was afraid to blink in case the air was full of splinters. There was not enough space on either side of the bed for both backpacks, so I put mine in the shower, which was also mostly made of wood. It cost ten lire more than *Psycho Pension* and didn't include breakfast. I accepted the price immediately and didn't even haggle.

We collapsed onto the bed, which squeaked in disapproval.

"This is ..." I said, preparing another apology.

"The stream is nice," she said. "The other one wasn't next to the stream. Just near it."

We lay listening to that stream. It was loud. Really, annoyingly, gurgle-some and splashy. I hoped I'd packed my earplugs. After this, we'd return to Istanbul. That would be significantly louder. "I understand Hemin better now, don't you?" I asked.

"Definitely," she said. "I mean, I think I knew more about the Kurdish issue than you. But yeah, seeing it up close again, and what has become of Diyarbakır." She sighed. "I don't think it's Israel–Palestine hopeless, but while Erdoğan is in power, there's not much more they can do to further their cause."

"Still," I said. "I'm very happy we came. Even with all those awkward dolmus silences."

She slapped me on the arm. "Don't make fun of my neurosis. I didn't make fun of yours, you control freak."

"You can though, I mean, what else are neuroses for? A bit of neurosis is useful on an average Wednesday. I think that's the true test of a relationship: how good is the average Wednesday?"

"How good are our average Wednesday nights?" she asked.

It was Wednesday, I realised. "I'm not sure we've ever had an average Wednesday. Not yet anyway. We're all action. It's never boring. Even today when it threatened to be dull, I threw a wobbly."

"Threw a wobbly?" she repeated.

"Spat my dummy out?" I tried.

"Spat your dummy out? What are all these weird idioms?"

"I made a big scene, basically."

"Yeah, you did. When we get back to Istanbul, I think we should change some things. We're very good in the apartment," she said. "But it's only when we leave it, we learn new things about each other, like today." She frowned. "And we don't have many shared hobbies, do we? Or any, really? That could be a problem, couldn't it?"

"Travel, maybe?" I suggested.

"Yeah, but you can't do that much if you have a job or kids. When we get back to Istanbul, I want to do more things out in the world," she said. "Maybe we can find a shared hobby or two yet?"

20

Back in Istanbul, we were out for a walk—part of our plan to be more in the world, searching it for hobbies. "How do you feel about surprises?" Evelyn asked as we crossed sides of the street in search of shade.

"I had enough surprises lately."

"I mean, in general?"

"I identify as someone who enjoys surprises," I said, as if it was really rather good of me.

"Yeah, but you also identify as a vegetarian. Do you actually enjoy them?"

I took off my baseball cap and rubbed my head. "If I could like them, I'd like them."

"But you don't?"

"I feel I've been clear on this," I said. "It's probably related to my control and obligation issues. Like if someone buys me something or takes me somewhere, I'm then obligated to be grateful. Which doesn't leave me any choices."

"Oh," she said in a way that told me she had bought me something or was taking me somewhere I'd be obligated to be grateful for, and that would leave me with no choices.

She swerved us toward a tall man in front of a large,

wrought-iron gate at the end of İstiklal Avenue, Istanbul's most famous shopping thoroughfare.

"Evelyn and Adam?" the man asked.

"Istanbul Eats?" she asked.

"Istanbul-what-now?"

"Your salads," she shook her head. "You need to learn how to cook. For your Adulthood Project."

"I'm Oğuz," said the man, stretching out his hand. I shifted nervously on the spot, trying to enjoy the surprise but feeling myself at the precipice of a terrible, perhaps even sulky mood. What pulled me back was Oğuz's large, terrific face and shaggy-rug eyebrows. He was half a foot taller than anyone needed to be, half a foot taller than even he needed to be, it seemed, because he stooped slightly to the side. I had the urge to slip a beer mat under his foot.

"We'll just wait for the others," he said sweetly, as if he couldn't even entertain a world in which they'd be late.

A friendly, bubbly Canadian joined first. Then two women from France with limited English. Then Rose, an American in a headscarf, who'd been living in Sweden. Together, we walked the narrow lanes where shops spilled their goods out onto the sidewalk, watched over by silver-tongued salesmen trying to hook tourists with practised banter.

"Istanbul is a city of food," Oğuz said as he led us, his umbrella aloft. Not that he was the sort of man you could lose. He was too tall and ungainly and distinctive of face. "No one eats like us Turks. And today we are going to feast."

At each shop the staff expected us, laying out trays of tasters. We feasted on salty white cheeses, twenty different nuts (there really are that many), a sour cold soup (one was enough), a chicken dessert (one was too many), and a mussel —the first of my life—which tasted like tiny, subtle ocean. I wondered if they'd prepared it in our neighbouring street in Tarlabaşı.

I hung back whenever Oğuz asked us cuisine questions, looking at the floor as if back in math class. He got me eventually—as we snaked our way from a shop where everything was pickled, to one where everything was a very sugary delight. "What type of cuisine do you like to cook?"

Fortunately, the rest of the group were too far behind to hear. "Fried," I said, before realising this was not a valid answer. "Kentucky fried," I added. "Erm ... the deep south? Creole, mostly."

Please have no questions.

I'm sure he had them, but he was a nice man and knew I was bluffing. "Everyone," he said with a clap of his giant's hands. "I hope you liked the tour. Now it's time for the fun to begin. Let's cook."

"Fun?" I whispered to Evelyn.

"If you want to drink while you cook, no problem. You are welcome to buy it on the way."

Everyone but Rose bought wine or beer. "I don't drink anymore," she said, staying outside the shop, as I put several clinking plastic bags down at my feet.

"When did you stop?" Evelyn asked.

"When I converted last year."

I'd wanted to ask about the headscarf, but there hadn't been an opening. "Was it difficult to give it up?" I asked.

"Yes. I used to live a very substance-dependent life," she said, making it sound like a bad thing.

On the second floor of a nearby apartment building, a showpiece kitchen with separate stations was waiting. Oğuz helped us set fire to a pepper. That was fun. Evelyn and I worked side by side, but as we cooked, she edged me out with her aggressive, authoritative, dictatorial elbows. By the end of the first course, my only job was slicing things, my usual job when we cooked in Berlin. It isn't a job I do well. The only thing worse than bringing a knife to a gunfight would be bringing me holding a knife to a gunfight.

"Is this your first time in a Muslim country, as a Muslim?" Oğuz asked Rose, an hour and a half later. We were sat around the room's large central table, deep into our stash of booze and with just scraps of food left. Gluttony had forced me to undo the top button of my shorts.

"Yes," Rose said. She had high cheekbones and a sharp, precise nose. She had immaculate skin and would have done well selling her own soap at a farmer's market. "I was so excited to be here, to be around other Muslims, but then I had a really awful experience at the airport. I was there in my hijab and was the last person in the line, like the very last, so I saw that this didn't happen to anyone else. They took me into a room and questioned me. There was a security guy and a police officer. The police officer was friendly, but the security guy was really rude. They were asking me why I converted, and if I was on my way to fight for ISIS?"

Her bottom lip quivered. "It was horrible. I burst into tears. I didn't expect them to, you know, roll out the red carpet or something. But I also didn't expect them to profile me. Not here." There was still a tiny lilt of California in her accent.

"I'm sorry that happened to you," Evelyn said, refilling her wineglass.

"Yes, me too," said Oğuz as he offered around the last of the tiramisu. "Have you read the Q'uran?" In most people's mouths, this would have been a loaded question, but Oğuz disarmed it somehow.

"Yes." She looked down at the countertop. "I mean, no, not all of it."

"Did it move you?" he asked.

"It did." She adjusted the front of her headscarf, hiding

a wisp of blonde hair. "But I've heard it's a completely different experience in the original Arabic. That in Arabic there's just these, like, oceans of meaning in every sentence that are untranslatable."

Oğuz frowned. "I've heard that too. It makes little sense to me, though. Why would God prepare his message so that it only works in one language?"

It seemed like a good point; the point landed. "The Turkish approach to Islam differs greatly from the Arabic," he said. "For us, everything is created by God. Every step you take, you are stepping on something God created. It's sacred. You don't need to go to some special building to feel connected to God."

I put down my empty can of beer. "If that's true, why is every second building in this city a mosque?"

"Well," he said with a smile, "when we go, it's nice to have choice." The group laughed. "If you look at the census, 95 per cent of Turks are Muslim, but only 15 per cent of us are strict Muslims, teetotal, praying five times a day Muslims. Most of us, we pray maybe once a week and go out with our girlfriends and have a drink or two and still consider ourselves devout."

The good Muslim turned to the fridge to get me another beer. "But the culture is changing. Erdoğan is changing it. Redefining what it means to be a Muslim. And that's going to cause problems. Is already causing problems."

Somehow, I found space for that tiramisu. "Maybe cooking together can be our hobby?" Evelyn asked as we walked down the stairs.

"It's your hobby," I said. "And you're so many years and cookbooks ahead of me, I'll never catch up. I'm just happy to know what a fig is and be able to make a passable salad. You keep cooking, I'll keep eating."

"Who said your salads are passable?" she joked.

"They're most just more-is-more. Not everything goes with everything, you know?"

"Well, it should," I said. "And I will make it so. Nothing must be excluded. No ingredient left behind." My voice was full of wonder. "It is not the ingredients who must change, it is us." I wobbled as I stepped back out to the street, momentarily blinded by the light and made unsteady by all the booze. "That was fun," I said. "I'm grateful. I think. Mostly because we met nice people. But still ..."

"See," she said proudly.

"Don't do it again."

21

"Rose," I said as we waited to cross the two wide roads between the cooking school and Tarlabaşı. Their crossing lights never worked, so we had to get across by intimidation: a group of pedestrians swelling and eventually growing large enough that dared spring off the pavement, forcing our way across en masse to the angry sound of cars braking and tooting their horns.

"I'd like to know more about her story," I said. "You never meet people going from atheist to religious."

"I bet she met a guy," Evelyn said.

"Why do you think that?"

"Come on," she said, as if it was my first day here and I still had a lot to learn. "And what makes you think she'd want to tell you her story anyway?"

I laughed. "I know from the old memoir-writing days that people always, always want to tell their story. Usually, you can't shut them up. They chase you and shout it out."

"Really?" she said. "Well. Prove it."

* * *

The next evening, just across the water in Beyazıt, part of the city's historical quarter, standing at the corner of the Grand Bazaar—home to a labyrinth of over four thousand shops—a modestly dressed Rose was waiting for us, ready to tell her story.

We took a seat in a gaudy shisha bar heavily adorned with ornate silver decorations. A giant red and silver shisha pipe was placed before us. A hospitable, smiling waiter placed hot, flaking red charcoal coals onto foil. The smell of sweet apple filled the air as the waiter handed me the pipe. The girls were probably used to this by now—that I was always the default.

"When are you leaving?" I asked Rose.

"Tomorrow."

"For where?"

"I'm moving to Qatar."

"Why the hell would you want to go to Qatar?" I said, and this hurt her, so I tried to back-pedal. "I mean, I've never been."

"It's a long story," she said.

"We've all evening."

"Okay, but where should I start?"

"Your faith?" I said, finding it difficult not to be distracted by even her simple black headscarf. "I've met plenty of people on the belief highway coming the other direction, but few going from secular to religious."

"Me too," she said, nodding. "If it hadn't happened to me, I think I would have been super judgemental about it. I thought religion was just like comfort for ignorant people."

I took the end of the pipe in my hand, pushed the plastic nozzle onto it, forgot if I was supposed to suck or blow, guessed blow, was wrong, then coughed embarrassingly.

"When did you convert?" Evelyn asked.

"Six months ago."

I handed the pipe to Evelyn, wheezing slightly from my gaffe. "Were you spiritual before that?" I just about managed to ask before coughing into my hand.

"Erm. *No.* I guess? Maybe? I mean, I did the typical white girl stuff, like a lot of yoga and loosely reading Buddhist philosophy and thinking I'd got it all figured out, you know? I thought religion was to comfort the stupid, but I was also desperately seeking comfort, like, all the time. There's this comedian Marc Maron who talks about the God-shaped hole. I was trying to fill that with all kinds of things and substances. Then I realised, well, you can actually fill the God-shaped hole with God."

"I notice you have this certain tone when you say *substances*," I said, adopting a slower, more measured tone. Maybe I wanted Evelyn to see me as a journalist; a professional; a man of precision. Someone in the world doggedly attempting to separate its fact from its fictions.

"I do?" she checked with herself. "Huh, yeah, probably. I think I had a bit of a problem in the past with substances. A weed problem, mainly. University was a blur of hanging out and getting high and drinking. I think it's because the alternative is actually feeling things. Really having to sit silently with yourself, you know?"

Evelyn smiled at me. I remembered she believed I was one of these people—that I could sit silently with myself, and I think she was right, before I met her. Now, my mind was a full blender with no lid whipping up a lust and fear smoothie.

The pipe continued its slow orbit of the table; us taking turns to clip in, inhale, feel the soft taste of burnt apple on our lips, exhale, pass it on, everyone keen not to take too much, nor to have it for too long.

"And so, after grad school, I had this friend who lived in

Sweden. She said she could get me a job teaching there. I went. It was great. Lovely people, a good job, but I still wasn't happy. I had this strong feeling that this can't be it, you know? Just thinking about when I'm going to buy the next vintage dress, or drink the next craft beer, or post the next picture on Instagram?" She paused, her mouth twisting left, then right. "This is where the story gets boring." Her head dropped. "Because then I fell in love with somebody. A Muslim man. Which is what everyone thinks must have happened, and it happened." She raised her hands protectively. I expected Evelyn to turn and give me a I-told-you-so glare, but she didn't. She wasn't that kind of person. And I don't think she wanted to be right about this; she just was.

"But I'm not with that person anymore," Rose continued. "And it was my choice completely to convert."

She composed herself and pulled her headscarf forward a little. "But I also can't say he wasn't the most important factor. I fell in love with this man who was the most interesting person I'd ever met." She was growing more animated as she talked, her chest bobbing, her speech accelerating. "He grew up in Syria. But he's ridiculously well educated. He never loses at chess, ever, to anybody. Speaks four languages fluently. Is a teacher. Children love him. No, adore him. But he's also this deeply spiritual person with a strong faith and a unique, critical view of everything because he's lived in both the Western world and the Arab world. I fell in love with him like beyond what I ever thought possible."

"Was there an age gap between you?" Evelyn asked.

Rose nodded. "Yeah, he's eight years older."

A waiter came and swapped out the charcoal. "He's a very convincing person, a great debater. And he has a very strong view that Islam is the right path for humans."

"And he encouraged you to study it?" Evelyn probed.

She considered it. "No, well, sometimes he might show me a video about love and Islam or recommend a particular scholar. But that wasn't it." She shook her head emphatically. "It was last summer. I went travelling through Europe with a bunch of friends. We'd been planning it for such a long time, and it was great, just really, really great, you know? But I just kept having that same feeling: is this it? I'm swimming in the beautiful azure Mediterranean Sea with my best friends, I'm drinking champagne in France, I'm checking all the boxes of my imagined life, and still I felt this emptiness. And I saw the emptiness in my friends too."

"Doesn't everyone have that, though?" I asked. "From time to time? Religious or atheist? A kind of perpetual underwhelm?"

"This is different. I remember ..." Her eyes glazed over. "I remember this perfect night in France, right? Perfect conversation. Perfect food. Perfect desserts eaten while watching these perfect, beautiful French people air-kissing each other and sipping cocktails in Toulouse. Just perfect." She paused, emphasising the perfection. "Then on the way home, my friends were like, *let's stop at this dive bar*. This shitty bar ... sorry, excuse my language." She looked around, embarrassed. "I try not to swear anymore. This shitty dive bar. And I was like seriously guys, wasn't that enough? Wasn't it enough? I went home and called him."

She still hadn't used his name.

"And I said, 'You're the best person I've ever met, and the most challenging person I've ever met, and I want to marry you.' He said no, of course. He said he could never marry me because I didn't even have faith. Any faith. Not even Christianity. I cried uncontrollably, not just about that, but about the night and about the sadness and about the hole. I felt at my wit's end, and he said, 'Rose, I think you should pray.'"

Evelyn's eyes narrowed. We were hearing the same story, but she was reacting differently to it. She was also leading the questioning now. "How long were you dating him when he said he couldn't marry you because you didn't have faith?"

"About two years."

"How come he could be in a relationship with you for two years, even though you didn't have faith?"

"He ... we weren't." She lowered her eyes. "Well, we were. He said we weren't. He never told his friends about us, or his parents."

"But you told yours?"

"Yeah."

"And it was a sexual relationship?" Evelyn asked.

Rose took a deep breath, but one not full of apple-scented shisha. "*Yes*. He had a way of justifying that. Of justifying everything. He was brilliant. Really. I wish you could meet him."

Evelyn's posture had stiffened. Tea arrived. We hadn't ordered it. Its appearance surprised no one.

"Anyway," Rose continued, "I thought that was a great idea. The praying. So, I tried it. And, well, it wasn't like *ooh something spoke to me*, but it was, sort of, like ... my heart spoke to me? It said, *Rose, you know what you need to do, just start doing that*. So, I did. We still had like two weeks left of that European holiday and they thought it was really weird, but I just completely stopped drinking. I think that's really the night I converted."

"But why Islam?" I asked. "It sounds like it could have been any religion?"

"I just feel Islam is a very pure religion. It offers like a science of living. It answers all of your questions. I mean, it's alienating, you know, it's scary to read it. But then there're moments where it feels unlike anything else. I think you need to have a scholar and a spiritual guide with you to start, because otherwise you'll get lost. That's how you get ISIS."

Evelyn drank the last of her tea. "And how have you interpreted it?"

"It's simple. We believe that the prophet, peace be upon him, lived in the most perfect way. The more we can emulate him, the more fulfilled we will be. That's it. For me, it's like stumbling around blind my whole life, then suddenly being given this lens I can use to see everything through."

"And you also get an afterlife, which must be pretty cool?" Evelyn joked.

Rose leaned forward. "It so is! That's just not something I believed until now, which is so weird to talk to new people about and not sound like a weird, crazy religious girl. But it's how it is. It's awesome to believe that. I thought my family would be mad when I converted. But my stepdad, I could cry just thinking about it, he just looked at me with the sincerest love and said, 'We support you, of course we support you.' And these are like, you know, conservative Midwestern, white Americans. They were so lovely. In most of the Western world, Muslims are the bad guy. I think it's because this is such a powerful religion. There's a good reason that people in power would try to villainise something that liberates people."

"Do you feel liberated?" Evelyn asked.

"Absolutely," she said, without hesitation. "We all need something to get through the day. Islam is just, well, a really beautiful way to get through the day."

"Can I hug you?" I said when we were back on the street, about to part, after several hours of wonderful, sincere conversation. She looked at the floor. "I'd rather you didn't."

"Oh, okay," I said, taking an awkward half step backwards.

Evelyn reached for her hand. "Good luck. You're brave."

We walked the forty-five minutes home. It was late for this part of town and the tourists retreated to their hotels. Our time in Istanbul was ending. I noticed us walking more intentionally, soaking up more of what we saw. "That was magical," I said, high on intimacy.

Evelyn slipped her arm around my waist. "It was. And you were right. She had a great story to tell. And she wanted to tell it."

"I think she wouldn't have told it like that, not so candidly, without you being there."

"We're a great team," she said. "I think you could have been a journalist, you know."

My chest almost burst with pride. "I tried, but I was just never quite able to shake the belief that I'm the better story, no matter the story. I wasn't a humble man in my twenties. I'm still working on that. People are definitely our shared hobby."

"They're the best drug," she said. "I really liked her, although I think she's kidding herself if she doesn't think she converted with the hope he'd marry her. She always talked like it was love, but it sounded like blind devotion or worship. She had him up on this pedestal and couldn't see any hypocrisy in how he was behaving."

"Do you think he was a hypocrite?" I asked.

"One hundred per cent," she said with hesitation. "One hundred. This story. Older guy, younger girl?" she lowered her voice. "This is not a relationship, but it's all the parts of relationships that I want, not the bits you want. We can have sex, but I won't tell my friends or family about you? *Please*." She groaned. "Such a common story."

"It was a great story."

"It's not a story, it's her life."

I nodded. "Sure, sure."

"No, don't do that." She stopped and pointed back towards the shisha lounge. "She really did date that man. Was tricked by that man. Will now have to live in Qatar."

"I know." I sighed. "I know. What do you think she'll make of it?"

"I think that she'll see a side of Islam so restrictive for women it'll take too much mental gymnastics to keep her faith in it."

We crossed onto Galata Bridge as the last tram of the night trundled away, and one of the pier's popular mackerel stalls lowered its shutter. Out on the water, little splashes of light bobbed from the few ferries still running back and forth. I'd most remember this bridge, those ferries, and that view. This city had grandeur.

"What do you think she thinks about us?" I asked. We'd shared our story to Rose, of course, albeit in less forensic detail.

Evelyn stopped, panic rising in her voice. "Are we like them?"

"What?" I spluttered. "No."

"Aren't we though?"

"Are you joking? There's no age gap between us. And I am not preying on you. Not taking anything from you you don't want to give."

She looked behind us again, back towards Eminönü. Süleymaniye Mosque dominated the skyline as usual from its perch on the hill, lit up like a giant nugget of gold. "She would have said the same," Evelyn argued. "You don't call me your girlfriend? Or like only ever by accident."

I tried to remember the last time I had referred to her as

my girlfriend. It was probably with the shoe-shyster on the first night. "It's an ordinary word. We're not ordinary."

She bristled. "I like ordinary. I want ordinary. We haven't even met each other's families. I'm giving ultimatums about having children and I've not even met the rest of the genes they would inherit."

"You don't believe in ultimatums," I joked, but she was somewhere else. She tilted her head. "No boyfriend has ever introduced me to his parents. Weird, right? Or maybe it's because I'm weird?"

"You're not weird. Well," I said, shrugging. "No weirder than everyone else."

I sat down on a bench and rubbed my head—my stress tell. "I don't understand why you would compare us to them? We're not like them."

"Okay," she conceded, sitting next to me. "I guess we're not in many important ways."

"There are so many important ways now, right?" I said.

"What do you mean?"

"Everything got heavy. Even that conversation was heavy. It was great too, but it was also sad and heavy. We are heavy now too. With all the decisions we have to make? Kurdistan was heavy. Different heavy, but heavy."

She shrugged. "Life is quite heavy for most people."

"It wasn't for me," I said. "You sort of made it heavy. First you made it light and exciting, but then you made it heavy."

"Can you stop saying heavy?"

"Mmm, I can try?" We sat watching a group of seagulls attack both each other and a full bin. There was a waft of urine from a secluded corner of the bridge, near the last fisherman casting his rod over the side. In the daytime, there were dozens.

"This is not my fault," she said. "It's happening to me,

too. You don't know what it's like to be a woman. To be a commodity. To know that you are losing value each year."

"A commodity?" I said sarcastically. "That really how you feel?"

She considered it. "Sometimes, yeah? More here than in Germany. And maybe more since I got the bad fertility news. I know now that my body is not as young as I thought it was, and yet it's not fulfilled the function that a lot of the world thinks it's here for."

"I don't think that, though."

"No," she said, smiling. "You think it's here for your pleasure."

I matched her smile. "I also think it's here for your pleasure." The ice between us was melting. "We are not like them," I said, again. "I'm going to buy a chess set." I said, looking up at the sharp hat that sat on top of Galata Tower, sure that it reminded me of a particular chess piece, one I would soon know the name of. "Maybe chess can be our new hobby?"

She chuckled. "I will destroy you. You're not strategic, as proven by your salads."

"Do you even know how to play chess?" I asked.

"No. But after I learn, I will destroy you."

"I know you will," I said, standing up and reaching for her hand. "Let's go home."

22

With just a week left of the trip, it was a lazy Saturday morning in bed. "There's a hike today," I said. "A group I found on Facebook. Maybe hiking could be our new hobby? It's very adult. Maybe a bit too adult?"

"I enjoy hiking," Evelyn said. "We already hiked together in Aralık."

"That was ..." I probed my feelings about that day. "Eventful."

I read the event description aloud—it was poetic and waxed lyrical about how cities steal our soul and crush our dreams and we must flee, flee to the safety of ... I don't know, lichen, moss, squirrels?

"It'll get us out and we'll meet people," she said. "So, yeah, let's do it."

We scrambled up and into clothes, threw water bottles into backpacks and were soon on the street, buying simits, the tough, ever-present rings of bread that would probably grow on trees here if they hadn't ripped them all up.

We descended into the mouth of the city's new subway system. In Berlin, the stations were so near the surface it felt like you could knock on the ceiling and people on the street would stop and look down. Here, the subways were huge, cavernous, endless, requiring a five-minute escalator ride just to reach the platform.

Forty-five minutes later, we took a long escalator up and walked to a bus station. "Are you the hiking group?" I asked the young people clustering together pensively, looking for a bus they didn't trust would come.

"You just made it," said Mohammed, a heavy-set young man with a squishy, bear-like face, and leather jacket. There were two men and two women with him, all of which deferred to him, I noticed. It's the sort of thing men notice.

"How far is it?" I asked.

"An hour or two."

In Berlin, I could bike ten minutes and be far enough into the woods to lose phone signal. This city was endless. The bus arrived. We sat together at the back. "Where are you from?" I asked Mohammed.

"Palestine."

"But you can travel?"

"I have a Pakistani passport."

"That's lucky."

He laughed. "Yeah, I have the third worst passport in the world, instead of the worst."

There's something relaxing about confident men, and Mohammed was a confident man; a man going to return our souls to us. "Are you from Istanbul?" I asked our co-hikers, all but one of which looked to be Turkish.

"Yes, but sorry, my English is not so good," said Z, a native Istanbuler with a precise, manicured, narrow goatee. He nodded at the Turkish girl sitting across the aisle. "She also."

"And you?" Evelyn asked the one that clearly wasn't a native—a blonde woman with pale skin and heavy freckles.

"Russian," she answered, then introduced herself as Marina.

"You don't meet so many Russians here," I said.

"No." She hesitated. "Well, I don't tell Turks I'm from Russia because they assume I'm a prostitute."

"Where do you say you're from?" Evelyn asked, as I wondered how many changing rooms the poor girl had hid in lately.

"Luxembourg."

"Why Luxembourg?"

"They don't know where it is."

Two hours later, the bus dipped over a hill and revealed a wide, flat azure sea. "We're still in Istanbul," said Mohammed. "Crazy, right?"

"I can breathe better," said Z.

"My soul," said Marina.

"Is good," added Ceda, the young girl with the supposedly bad English, as she took out her phone for a bus selfie —lips pushed forward, two-finger peace sign over her chest.

The bus dropped us next to the water. There wasn't a beach, just sharp, precise cliffs. The group cheered, and we posed for a group photo. "We free now," said Z, who smiled a lot but said little.

We walked. Or perhaps hiked. "How long are you going to stay in Istanbul?" I asked Marina.

"I don't know."

"You like it so far?"

She bit her cheek. "It's not always easy here as a woman alone."

"How is your Turkish?" I asked.

"It doesn't exist."

Evelyn was up ahead, talking to the Turkish girl, Ceda, who wasn't talking back. I knew what this would mean:

Evelyn would talk more, rushing to fill the gaps with her stories and anecdotes.

"And your Turkish?" Marina asked.

"Barely a word," I said. "Evelyn speaks it, I think. Germans are funny with foreign languages. They don't speak until they know they can do so perfectly. The odd word is not enough. It has to be full, grammatically correct sentences."

"Russians too," she said, laughing. "We're perfectionists."

"Germans are masochists."

"What are Brits?" she asked.

"Too kind to themselves."

Z swerved us from the empty, narrow coastal road. Soon we were picking our way through an overgrown field, grass to our knees. The group cheering as if we were explorers charting a distant, unicorn-filled land. The field became a thicket, the thicket an impenetrable wall of spikes that forced us back onto the road. "Did you research a route?" I asked Mohammed, who had retaken the lead from Z.

"*No*. We just make it up as we go."

"Are there hiking trails here?" I asked.

"Not really. No one hikes."

"They drive and picnic next to car," said Z. We passed a heap of polystyrene boxes in a clearing near chestnut trees. "I hate that about this place," he said, kicking the boxes deeper into the brush while scowling.

Forty-five minutes later, we stopped in a wooded area perhaps thirty metres from the road's edge. Mohammed removed the tent from his backpack and laid it out on the ground.

"Tea?" Z asked, starting a tiny fire. We were on a scratchy, uneven bit of land. It was five minutes through rocky terrain to the cliffs and the sea. We drank our tea and then wandered, scratching at the land like chickens. "I'm not sure these people are hikers," Evelyn said as she joined me at the cliff edge.

"How long do you have to walk before something is a hike?" I asked.

"Half a day, at least."

"How long did we walk?"

"I want to say max one hour? I think they just like camping amongst trees."

Ceda joined us. "Photo?" she asked.

I took her phone. She struck a series of seductive poses: lifting her arms above her head, rotating her face left and right, blowing a kiss, sticking her chest out to present her breasts as if in a shop window. Her hair was lustrous, black and shimmering. She was undeniably beautiful. I zoomed out, making her small and the sea huge. I returned her phone, and we walked back to camp together.

A few minutes later, she began whispering to Mohammed. "Ceda wants to ask you a question," he said, playing translator. "You are a couple, yes?"

We both nodded. I'd assumed this was obvious, although we were careful with public displays of affection outside of Beyoğlu.

"Are you married?" he asked, or rather she asked, via him.

"No," I said.

"But you live together?"

"Yes," Evelyn said. "Well, kind of? It's a bit of a test. Anyway." She nodded. "Yes."

The group murmured about this scandal. "When are you going to get married?" Z asked.

Evelyn's mouth narrowed. "No one in Berlin gets married. It's not really important, marriage. Barely a thing."

"Boyfriend and girlfriend," Ceda said, in English, trying

the words out. She swapped back to Turkish. "Your parents are okay with this?" Mohammed translated.

"Sure. I mean, we haven't met each other's parents yet," Evelyn said, finishing the last of her tea.

"You haven't met each other's parents?" said a disbelieving Mohammed, who turned to check the others were understanding, offering a brief translation for Z and Ceda. "Crazy."

"But you're old," said Marina. "To not be married?"

"What do you mean, we're old?" Evelyn asked after a severe case of the bristles. "How old do you think we are?"

The group consulted. "Thirty?"

"We're thirty-four," Evelyn said.

The group received this figure as if it were news of an impending, terrible rain shower: heads lowered and shook, Z dragged a stick through the ground, Mohammed removed a shoe and shook out dirt, Marina swished the kettle in the air before returning it to its stick over the fire. Their reaction was remarkable to watch. It was like looking in a funhouse mirror. While I believed myself to be a reasonably fit thirty-four-year-old, the image of me being reflected off them was of a decrepit eighty-four-year-old, minutes from death and yet still an unmarried, childless bachelor.

"How old is everyone here, then?" I asked.

"Twenty-three," said Mohammed.

"Twenty-one," said Z.

"Twenty-two," said Marina, lowering her eyes.

I sat down heavily, forgetting to check the ground. "Ouch," I said about the pine cone I'd just sat on. I threw it away in anger. "We're the oldest here by ten years?" I was feeling things, many things, and not only because of the pine cone. They were tangling up all these feelings. Knotting in my stomach like emotional yarn. How could it be strange that two people are perfectly happy having sex with

191

each other repeatedly, without the involvement of their government or parents, and without signing a contract stipulating that they will only have sex with each other but no one else, forever, or rather, until death does them part? This group's surprise was extra jarring, and so conflicting-feeling-inducing, because they were so much younger than us, and so I expected them to think like us. Or more progressively, even.

Only Ceda had not said her age. "How old are you?" Evelyn asked her. Ceda tried to hide behind her hands. "Oh, come on. We all said it," Evelyn encouraged.

"I'm embarrassed," she whispered.

"She nineteen," said Z.

Ceda hit him playfully on the shoulder. "Old, I know."

"Are you even studying yet?" I said and immediately regretted. Not everyone wants to study, which is something I forgot.

"My family wants me to ..." she checked with Mohammed for a word, "*marry* soon."

"You can pick here, right?" I asked. "Who you want to marry?"

"Yes." She hesitated. "Well ... they have someone. But I can say too."

"You like him?" Evelyn asked.

She shrugged. "I not know."

"Are you allowed to date?" I asked. "To have boyfriends? To have sex?"

Mohammed nodded. So did Z. Ceda simply laughed. It was clear the laugh meant no; there were different rules for her.

"That's part of why I moved here," said Marina, pushing a stick through the ground. "I was working in Sweden but lost my job. I was going to go back to my village in Russia, but my parents told me not to bother because I'm twenty-two, so no one will marry me. I'm too old now."

"Seriously?" I asked.

Evelyn tutted, not at what we were being told, but at my disbelief of it. "Seriously," Marina said, as I looked pityingly at Ceda. As far as her culture was concerned, she was at her peak? A woman who had never studied, probably never left Turkey, never lived away from her parents? While in Russia, at twenty-two, they considered Marina wilting? I didn't even want to think about Evelyn, at the autumnal age of thirty-four.

"Commodity," I said, under my breath.

We strung a net between trees. A game of low-stakes volleyball took place. "My ... what's it called?" Z asked.

"Serve," I said.

"She served."

"I serve."

"He serve." They took turns cycling pronouns joyfully. "I not serve you," said Mohammed, and they laughed hysterically.

"It's out," I said when Mohammed's serve was so long it bounced off a tree and rolled down a hill.

"More than out," said Z, "out of Istanbul, out."

They howled and cackled. Mohammed pretended to serve but scooped the ball under his baggy T-shirt. The laughter was cacophonous. We got swept up in it too, although mostly out of politeness. I realised that when you don't share language, humour becomes slapstick. Next time he served, I tried to head it back. I missed, and the ball hit my nose and knocked off my glasses.

"It is out," said Z as the ball dropped onto the line we'd scratched into the sand.

"It was in," Marina argued.

"You are in." This made no sense, but they giggled and giggled.

"Point," he said.

"What is your point?" she asked.

Evelyn dropped out, sitting and watching quietly from the sidelines. I knew what she was thinking: there are many types of friends. If we stayed here, these would work. But they would always be friends of necessity—a group huddling together to not be lonely apart. They were making the best of each other. Just as we were all making the best of this scrubby piece of land, pretending it was a wilderness, an Eden, a place we had hiked to, even though we could still hear cars passing on a nearby motorway. These people are nice people, but they're not our people. We had a little tribe, but they were all back in Berlin. Finding new members here had proved difficult. Partly that was a language problem, partly it was age, culture, and outlook. Soon it wouldn't matter, because soon we'd be home.

A few hours later, we said goodbye and walked back to the road with Ceda. It was a long journey back to the apartment. Three hours, at least. At the bus stop, at Ceda's request, I took her photo for the last time; two victory signs now. The bus was full and so she sat away from us.

I glanced over at her. "What's going to happen to her, do you think?"

Evelyn waited a beat. Her mouth narrowed. "She'll marry that man and they'll make babies and she'll be their mother and his unofficial mother and not much else, probably."

"It's a waste," I said.

"It is, yeah."

23

I leaned back in the cafe's chair, cracked my knuckles, and pondered how I was going to spend the afternoon. Evelyn had joined the A2 Turkish course, even though we'd have left before the exam. It was her hobby, and I enjoyed having half of each day apart. It made me appreciate the afternoons more.

My phone rang; it was her. "So ... well, you know Leanne from my course?"

"The Dutch girl?" I'd heard stories about her but had never met her.

"Yeah. Can she stay at ours for a few days?"

"Sure. Why?"

"She's being harassed by her sleazy landlord. She doesn't feel safe there anymore."

"*Oh*. Well, of course."

It went quiet while she checked something. "She also needs someone to be there when she meets him for the key handover. Do you think you could do it?"

"I ..." I hesitated. "Is he, er ... violent?"

She asked Leanne. "She doesn't think so. Just very, very sleazy."

"I can do it," I said, without knowing if I could, while also mentally reserving the right to run away and hide from it, if necessary.

"You're the best," Evelyn said.

"When?" I asked.

"Meet us in an hour at Taksim, by the simit place?"

"There's a million simit places—"

The line went dead. I scratched at my chin as, outside, one of the historic white and red trams rolled up İstiklal Avenue. A shyster shoe cleaner dropped his brush, but too late. The tourist he was trying to ensnare ignored it. He waited a few seconds, then crept back for it, disappointment on his disingenuous face. Opposite was a Turkish delight shop that also had ice cream, and a vendor was putting on an elaborate show for a tourist, somewhere between slapstick and magic, using his serving stick to perform slight-of-hand as he moved the cone and ice cream back and forth, swapping and twirling amongst different cones. I smiled, watching it, remembering how entertained I'd been when he'd done it to me in the first week.

I sipped from my mocha; it was okay. I thought I could learn to like it, maybe, if I drank twenty more. I could drink twenty more? It would make me very jittery, perhaps, but that might be a good thing when confronting a sleazy landlord, right?

Thoughts rolled in and out like a tide, and I splashed around in them until it was time to meet the girls. I went to the simit stand—red, white, and gold, movable with its three bicycle wheels but made heavy by a mountain of stacked, dense bread being sold at giveaway prices—that we'd frequented most often together, on the corner of İstiklal and Siraselviler. The seller nodded at me, recognising me as a regular customer, and I dipped into my pocket for a coin.

The girls arrived. Leanne was like a younger Evelyn: a

pretty blonde with big, blue, meerkat eyes. In this part of the world, a blonde is a great trophy. Turkish is a macho culture: men are men and women are conquests. A place of simmering aggression and where if the choice is losing face or getting in someone's face, you pick the latter.

"Hi," I said, hugging Evelyn. "How was class?"

"Good," she said. Leanne thumbed her backpack's straps and looked at the ground. "Thank you for helping me," she said, her voice quiet and apologetic.

I offered them some simit. "I, er ..." I cleared my throat. "How much help do you need? What's happening?"

She looked up. "Did Evelyn tell you about my fiancé?"

"Briefly," I said to hide that she'd actually told me in great detail, even though it was a story you only needed to hear the start of to know its predictable end. On a family holiday to Turkey, Leanne had got to know her waiter. They'd only spent a little time together but had somehow fallen in love, and whenever she could visit him, she did. He worked six days a week for a few hundred euros a month. On the last trip he'd proposed, and she'd said yes. "He has another woman," she said, dropping her eyes back to the pavement. "The engagement is over."

"And your landlord?" I asked.

"I was mostly here to learn Turkish and wait for my fiancé to find work in Istanbul. So ..." she rubbed her hands together. "I'm done. And my landlord's getting creepier and creepier." She looked around, as if he might lurk behind any of the four simit, two roasted chestnuts, and a Burger King that flanked us. A black cat strolled past, which I told myself wasn't an omen. I stepped back to get out of the way of the crowds flowing past us.

"A woman alone in Istanbul. It's ..." She hesitated. "Tiring."

"I think it's best if I don't come," Evelyn said. "It'll look like an ambush."

"Are we ambushing?" I asked.

"I just need to meet him one last time," Leanne said. "To hand the key over and have him check the apartment and return the deposit. I need that money for my flight home."

"Okay," I said. "Let's go."

As Leanne and I walked towards her apartment, I noticed how differently she moved to Evelyn. Evelyn moved quickly here, keeping her eyes low, saying no by default to anything offered—directions, food, tea, to practice Turkish with school children, to visit a gallery—then and only then, as she was already moving away, did she consider if the answer to it was actually yes? If it was, she'd go back.

Leanne wasn't like that. Well, at first she was, but I chalked that up to the awkwardness of her needing my help. Once she had that, and had met me, she transformed, shoulders back, head up, taking it all in.

It was a twenty-minute walk to a quiet, residential area on the edge of Şişli, one of the upscale neighbourhoods.

"Who does he think I am?" I asked at the door, trying to radiate the calm I didn't feel.

"Tell him you're a friend visiting from Germany. If you're not there, there's no way he'll give me the deposit back." Her voice choked with emotion. "Well, not without stuff, awkward stuff."

"When are you leaving?"

"In two days."

"What's he like?"

She looked away. "It's ... hard to explain. It's not overt, exactly," she said, shuddering. "I'm scared of him. At the start it was just texts, but now he turns up at the apartment unannounced. And he has his own keys."

We walked up a narrow flight of stairs into her first-floor apartment. It overlooked a small graveyard which had enough trees and space to count as a park in Istanbul. The apartment was small and interestingly cut, with low, angled ceilings, a small kitchen, and a larger combined living room/bedroom; perfect for one person.

It was quiet, genuinely, exotically quiet. I soaked in it as I waited, sitting at the circular wooden table next to her bed while Leanne busied herself packing the last of her things into her suitcase.

I challenged myself to move as little as possible. I wanted to appear at ease, hiding the snake of dread slithering up from the pit of my stomach. Time was sluggish, clunky, unapologetic; not that they valued punctuality in these parts.

I realised she'd not told me his name. "What's his—"

He inserted his key into the lock. The door opened. A small man in a crisp white shirt, black circular glasses, and with a neat goatee entered. He looked more the philosopher than the brute, and seeing this, I relaxed a little.

"Hi," he said, poking his head into the kitchen. He noticed me through the open door. "And where is my dear Leanne?"

"Hi," I said, standing up. "She's in here."

Leanne walked over to the door he now filled. He leaned in and kissed her on a cheek she gave reluctantly before going red and slinking back towards her suitcase.

"And who are *you* then?" he asked.

I shook his hand. "Adam."

"He's visiting me," Leanne explained.

"How ..." he said, flashing all his very white, very straight teeth. "Nice?"

"Lovely place you have here," I said, sweeping a hand nowhere in particular and smiling like a moron.

"Yes," he agreed, turning to her. "It's a shame dear Leanne is leaving. Especially when we've been getting on so ..." he made a clicking noise from the side of his mouth, "well. Haven't we, dear Leanne?"

"Um-hm," dear Leanne mumbled as I sat back down. The table only had two chairs. He took the seat opposite me, putting his briefcase down onto the tabletop. Leanne sat to my right, perched on the edge of the bed. He opened the briefcase and ducked beneath it so obscuring his head. He waited a few seconds, then popped back up, his eyes peeking over the rim of the briefcase's lid. "I got you a gift," he said swiftly, then ducked into the briefcase again before peeking back over the rim. Slapstick was happening again. "A goodbye gift."

He pulled his head back and flipped the briefcase abruptly closed, revealing both himself and his open hand, a small Istanbul snow globe sitting in his palm.

"Oh. That's ..." Leanne thumbed her ear. "*Nice.*"

He handed it to her, a treacly grin on his face. "To remind you of the city. And of me, of course." He was beaming, proud of himself, sure he had done well.

She shook it, smiling weakly, as a chill worked its way down my spine. He met my eyes, awaiting my reaction to his gift. "Very kind," I said, almost apologetically. It fell silent as we all waited for each other to speak. He seemed to enjoy the silence.

"So," he said eventually, with a bounce of his eyebrows. "I've been a good landlord, yes?"

"Yes," she said without hesitation.

"You've no ..." He looked first at her, then at me. "Problems with me?"

"No," she said, her voice trembling.

"Good."

"Leanne tells me you're a very *fair* landlord?" I said.

"Of course." He nodded once. "It is a question of honour."

She leaned over and put the keys on the table. He looked annoyed at them, at this rushing of the proceedings. He pulled out some papers, then stopped, then put them back. "We'll stay in touch?"

"Of course," she said. With each sentence they passed back and forth, she seemed to shrink while he grew.

His voice rose. "I could visit?"

"Yes."

"When?"

"I need to ... get settled."

"Hmm," he snorted.

I looked down at my phone and shook my head. "We need to go soon, Leanne."

"I see," he said in a disappointed tone. He gave me an insincere grin. "And what do you do, Adam?"

"I'm a writer," I said, because it meant something in Turkey. Or it used to anyway.

"A writer," he whistled. "I would like to read your books one day. I'm a businessman." He pushed back his shoulders. "Apartments and a tea shop, a little import and export, of course."

"With your father, I heard?" I said to lance that growth.

He bristled. "Yes. We're the number one Erasmus landlord in the entire city."

I nodded and his eyes wandered from me back to Leanne, who was crossing and uncrossing her arms and legs. "I suppose you'll be wanting your deposit? Even though you're breaking the contract? And ending this ... *friendship* we're building?"

"Sorry," she said, keeping her eyes on the floor. "I mean, yes?"

He tapped his chin. "Why *are* you leaving so suddenly, dear Leanne?"

"Family issues," she lied.

He kept tapping, looking slowly around the room as I got my phone out again, frowning down at it, as if it had delivered yet more terrible news.

"You understand you are breaking the contract, though?" he asked.

She looked up from the floor. "Yes."

"Well," he took a deep breath. "Difficult situation then, yes?"

"It's lucky you're a man of honour," I said.

He stiffened. "I suppose, yes."

We waited. He moved to drumming his fingers on the table. "How soon do you think you'll be ready for visitors?"

"I-I'm not sure."

"I see." His eyes wandered over to the window, then wandered slowly back. "I can only give you half," he said. "The deposit."

Her mouth tightened. She gave a weak nod.

"Unless ..." he brightened, "maybe I could give you a little more? Since you're my favourite tenant. Did you know you're my favourite tenant, dear Leanne? Would you like that?"

"Oh," she said. "That's ... nice?"

"Yes. How much would you like that?"

"Sorry?"

"I'm just wondering."

"Oh." She faltered. "That would ... I need it."

He smiled, for he both knew this and was revelling in it. "I would just need to look around? To check the apartment is in good condition." He craned his neck back, looked over his shoulder. "The kitchen, for example?"

"I just cleaned it," she said.

"Perhaps you can come with me while I look?"

"O ..." she stood, slowly, "-kay?"

She let him go first, then followed, keeping the door to the kitchen open. I tipped my chair onto its left two legs and watched through the open door. It was not overt; she was right, but I saw it, perhaps for the first time: how men did this. Not all men, but some men; too many men. The kind of men that made women hide in changing rooms; stopped them from being able to hitchhike; saw them as commodities and conquests; pretended a woman was their girlfriend when she was their mistress; pretended a mistress would soon become their girlfriend; or told a woman they couldn't be with her because she was an atheist, while being with her when she was an atheist.

Here, with this man, it was about abusing power. Finding a point of leverage, then exploiting it to make a woman uncomfortable, pushing her boundaries bit by bit until they find the point where they say no, or ideally, make it so uncomfortable for them to say no that they don't dare. Make it easier for her to just to comply, to do this next thing, in order to get it all over with.

What's one more thing? And so, they give them that thing, and they can push for one more.

He opened the cupboard under the sink, then brushed his hand across the counter, moving closer to her, leaning in and whispering something in her ear, his hand moving down to touch her waist.

I leapt up and darted into the kitchen, my chair falling backwards against the bed. "We need to go, Leanne. Evelyn has landed. My girlfriend arrives today," I said. Evelyn was my girlfriend. It didn't matter what I thought about that word. It was simply the reality. A beautiful, challenging, interesting reality in which I was proud to call a woman like her an "ordinary" word like that. I ran a finger over the countertop appreciatively, "Ohhh," I enthused. "Look how clean it is in here. You did a great job, Leanne."

He took a small step away from her. "It's a shame to rush away. Perhaps you can all come back and drink tea with me later in my tea garden?"

She shuddered.

"Perhaps," I said, and planted my hands on my hips, staring into his face, holding eye contact until he looked away. It was a small kitchen and my body language let him know it was time for us to leave it. He pulled some money from his pocket, made a show of counting it out on the counter.

"I hope to see you again," he said.

"Yes."

"When?" he pleaded.

"I ... will write you?" she said, her disbelief and uncertainty accidentally making it a question.

"I will wait."

"Walk with me," he asked, once we were back down on the street.

"We're going the other way," I said without knowing where we were exactly. He leaned in to hug her. She leaned back, but accepted it, her body stiff and lifeless. He held out his hand, I shook it, and we both gripped as tightly as we could. I don't know how long we stood there—it could have been five seconds; it could have been fifty-five seconds.

"Goodbye, Adam," he said through clenched teeth.

"Goodbye, Mr Landlord."

We went different directions, but only made it around the next corner before Leanne fell against a wall, and in a series of sobs, let out some of what she had been holding in, perhaps for months. Yesterday, she thought she was in love and going to marry a Turkish man and build a life here with him. Today she was single, knew she'd been lied to, had narrowly avoided a predator (or more likely two predators), had no home, and had no idea what to do next with her life. She wiped away a tear and tried to compose herself. "It's not just me, right?"

I went to hug her, then stopped; she didn't know me either. Evelyn vouched for me, but no doubt Leanne would have vouched for her boyfriend until earlier this week. I stepped back. "That was ..." I balled my hands into fists. "He's good at it."

She nodded. "Yeah."

"There are a lot of men like him here?"

"You get hassled every day."

"I'm sorry."

She shrugged. "It's not so bad."

That didn't mean it couldn't be much, much better. "You excited to go home?"

"I'd leave right now if I could. Hang on," she said, opening the zip of her suitcase, pulling out the snow globe, and throwing it into the top of a bin. This was a sad day for her, yet I was giddy. All I could think was how extraordinarily lucky she was to get to leave this place, be free of her waiter, and soon be back in her own culture. Why would she want to live in this blossoming autocracy, married to a man who worked six days a week for €500 a month, with a passport she can't use, and no shared, fluent language?

It would have been a mistake, and now she didn't have to make it. "It's not really worked out, Turkey and me," she said. I nodded, knowing that it hadn't for us, either. Circumstances had changed—both in the city and in our relationship—and that had reduced the levity of our time here, pushed the city into the background. Which was okay.

Before this day, from Evelyn's stories of Leanne, I had only seen her as a naïve young girl tricked by a sleazy waiter who preyed on foreigners. But if you've never been tricked,

I realised, it's probably because you've not trusted. If you don't trust, you've missed out on dozens of wonderful experiences, enjoyed with the vast majority of humanity—who you can trust and are unabashedly terrific. She would trust again soon, I was sure, and would be rewarded for it.

We walked. And with that walk, slowly, a little lightness returned to her steps. We skipped down the hill to Tarlabaşı —a place full of people like her, people whose best-laid plans had collapsed to rubble and who were now busy rebuilding.

That night, Evelyn and I went to a football game. Leanne wanted to be alone so didn't join us. The game was unimportant. We were there to watch and be part of the crowd—an unrestrained, wild animal mass. Sport is one of the few places men can show unbridled emotion without being judged by other men, and I took advantage of that, letting out some of mine.

"What do you think of Leanne?" Evelyn asked as we walked towards Üsküdar to get the ferry home, passing the twelfth kebab restaurant in two minutes. A wall of yellow taxis waited on the other side of the road. "She's ... *young*?" I said. "I mean, that sounds like an insult. It's not an insult."

"Yeah, I think I know what you mean. She has this freshness, somehow? Naivete, but in a more positive form? Like you can only have when you're that young. I took a walk with her last week. We ended up in some artist's gallery. Then his friends came. Then we all went to a bar and smoked shisha." I waited for the story to turn bad. "It was great."

A cafe was closing up for the night, stacking its chairs. "I got to see something there today. It was a privilege, in a way."

"That's a strange way of looking at it."

"I know. But it's easy not to believe someone, you know?

To think they're exaggerating. But actually, it was worse than she said. She was almost defending his behaviour. Minimising."

She nodded, perhaps recognising that behaviour. "Those situations are rare. Well, kinda rare. Usually, you can get away. I've been thinking about that a lot today, actually. How I don't miss travelling alone. Being here with you, it's just so relaxing. I feel guilty for saying that, like it makes me a bad feminist or whatever, but it's the truth. It's not that I need you, just that I benefit from you."

I didn't want to make this about me. "She is impressive," I said.

"She is."

We looked out at the slow bobbing water of the Bosphorus, the lights of the ferries bouncing on its surface as we entered the ferry terminal. Isha, the last call to prayer, rang out. We stayed quiet, listening reverently, sitting on the hard plastic seats in the waiting area.

"I think I get it better now," I said when it was over. "The commodity thing. I thought you were exaggerating, but you're not. And it's not fair. Whatever you do, you get judged. For not wanting to be a mother, or how you mother, for sleeping around, not sleeping around, how you dress, how you act, your age, for wanting a career, for wanting equal pay. You're playing a game you can't win. I was naïve too, I think, about how different the female experience is." She took my hand, held steady eye contact, and let me talk. "And now I feel a pressure to understand it," I continued. "Because if we have a child, it might be a girl. I *want* it to be a girl; that would be more interesting to me. But then, I worry I won't be able to prepare her. Or protect her?"

"It's not as bad as you make it sound. Not in Germany, anyway. I can recommend some books. And I'll be there. And it's getting better."

"Books only get you so far, as you know from your child-hood. People are much weirder than books can ever prepare you for. And you might not be around." I frowned. "Something might happen to you. And then I'll be alone and maybe I'll make some crucial mistake and before you know it, she's lying at the bottom of a ditch or is broken-hearted on her way to Qatar."

She took a deep, melancholic breath.

"And the pressure you feel," I said before she could interject. "Every time I pick up the paper, another member of the Rolling Stones is having a child and they're like ninety-seven years old or something, and it doesn't matter." I shook my head. "For men, it never matters. Almost nothing matters. While you have your fixed number of eggs and about twenty-five fertile years, and then that's it."

"Yeah," she said. "That's it."

"I've been a dick."

"No." She raised her hands.

"I have."

"You haven't." She shook her head. "It's okay to be afraid. It's okay to need time. It's okay to want to test our relationship. To freak out and be irrational sometimes. You haven't judged me when I've done that. When I've almost had panic attacks in airports. Remember that?"

I laughed. "It's not something I'll forget."

"I'd be worried if you weren't worried because it would mean you weren't taking all this seriously. And you are. In your own way. I feel bad for putting you in this situation. But apologising," she said, smiling. "Trying to understand. That's just what I was saying after Chai Talks. I don't know many men willing to do that. Certainly no man I ever dated. And I'm not sure I've ever heard my father apologise to my mother."

"Really?"

"No. If we have a son one day, I would want him to move through the world like you do. Gently but firmly, somehow."

I shook my head. "I'm indecisive. And dithering."

"I've seen so many macho men in my life, honey. Politics is full of them. Every room just dripping in testosterone. Certainty is a red flag for me now. A turn-off. The world is so complex. Half the time we're just guessing. Groping around in the dark, you know?"

I laughed. "But I make no sense?"

"*Yes.* Exactly. That's the right answer. The honest answer. I make no sense either. I'm full of contradictions. I'm strong in some areas but so, so weak in others. I can argue for an hour in a room full of men about some small political point or decision, about the layout of a stupid flyer, but I'm terrified to send a WhatsApp asking if someone wants to go for a beer with me that evening. I believe so strongly enough in us I can imagine us having a family one day, but I panic every time we stop talking in case that means it's over, that all the magic's used up. And no matter how many self-help books I read, every time we argue, I just feel this incredible urge to flee. My emotions just completely overwhelm me, and I feel like I'm going to pop like a party balloon." She lowered her head. "No one makes any sense."

I burst into tears. "I'm sorry."

She wrapped me in a hug. People were looking. The timer counted down to zero. The ferry was here. "Hey, come on. There's nothing to apologise for."

I tried to pull myself together. This was not the place for tears, nor the culture. I stood up, took some deep breaths, wiped my eyes on the football scarf I was wearing. On the ride home, the water calm, and the nearly full moon casting shadows onto the water, Evelyn talked while we stared lovingly out at the night skyline, knowing we'd leave soon. That there wouldn't be many chances to enjoy this view. That even though we were shivering in the breeze, we wouldn't give in and move down from the open top deck.

Leanne was up when we were back. We had a nightcap on the terrace. "You're good together," I heard her say when I went to the toilet because our apartment was really, really tiny. "It's real, what you have. You're lucky."

"Yes," Evelyn said, "we are. And you will be too."

24

The first sharp crack of thunder split the air like an axe, wood. We cast furtive glances upwards. The clouds were growing ever darker since we'd left the apartment, and now, as we hurried towards Galata Bridge, they were the colour of wet cement.

"Could it be no one introduced you to their parents not because they're embarrassed of you, but the opposite?" I asked. I was open to a little rain, something to help shift the muggy heat.

She screwed up her face.

"Hear me out," I continued, as we jumped out of the way of a speeding bus cornering far too quickly. We were used to being nearly run over now; barely registered it anymore. "You're so exactly what my parents would want," I said. "What they would hope for in a daughter-in-law. If you then disappeared, I'd never hear the end of it."

Her tongue probed her mouth. "No, I haven't considered that because it's stupid."

"You should."

"Uh-huh. Right. Fine. Okay. Crazy man."

A taxi honked, hoping to drive us across the bridge. We

were on our way to watch dervishes whirl in ecstatic communion with their God; one of the last things on our Istanbul bucket list.

"So, I read that, while training," Evelyn said, changing the subject as the first drops of rain fell and we passed the anglers fishing over the teal-coloured railings of the bridge, "they keep their foot skin in a little bag to show how much they've practised. Now that's commitment, right? And the hats? There have been so many great headwear periods in human history, you know? Then we invented the baseball cap, and everyone just gave up." She stopped. "The tram is closed; that's a bad sign. I don't want to get caught in a storm in the middle of the bridge."

I tugged her arm. "It'll be fine. Come on."

She shook me off. "It's too open."

The rain intensified, becoming a thick curtain of water. I kept tugging. "I queued for an hour for these tickets. If there's a once-in-a-lifetime storm, we'll have a cracking view."

Reluctantly, she relented, and we hurried on, passing a stream of people coming in the opposite direction. The taxis were full now, no longer honking at us. The wind was so strong we bent against it, our heads down, as it tried to force us to the right, over the railing and into the Bosphorus, coughing and spitting angrily. It looked like you could surf on it, which wasn't very unusual.

We hurried on.

Then it happened ...

It happened in a blink.

It happened all at once.

That's how it always happens, I guess. How it jumps from *before* to *too late*. It might not have been God, but it was certainly biblical. Thunder roared; lightning strobed; hail and rain crashed down so heavily that it hurt, was so dense you couldn't see beyond your own nose. The wind was feral, wounded, and striking out at anything in its path, whipping the water up into great sheets of wet glass that smashed at our feet.

People screamed. We were in the middle of the bridge now. It made no sense to turn back. Pushing on, we desperately searched for somewhere to escape the water and wind, for somewhere to hide or at least tether ourselves.

We were too late. Everywhere was full, closed, closing—the safe spots all taken. "Where?" I shouted.

"I don't know," she said. "Down?"

"Okay," I yelled, holding the handrail with both hands as we fought our way down the stairs to the bridge's lower level. She was just behind me. We were near to where we'd had dinner on our first night. No one descended with us and that should have been a sign, a warning.

We missed it.

Just as I left the bottom step of the stairs, letting go of the handrail, the next wave lurched over the side and into us, spinning me almost off my feet. The wind, forced through an even narrower space, was actually stronger down here. I lunged for a pole in the centre of the concourse as the next wave built. Evelyn let go of the handrail and ran over to me. I wrapped her inside me as we interlocked our fingers around the pole. We adjusted the angle of our bodies, turning to get as much protection from the wind as we could, dropped our heads, and waited. The stormed raged on, the wind as loud as a punk concert, broken only occasionally by the sounds of people screaming.

For the first time since we'd nearly crashed our tuk-tuk on the last day in India, I considered the possibility that we might die together.

I found that I really didn't want to die.

I understand that no one wants to die.

But ...

Well ...

I like really, really didn't want to die. The last weeks had been full of revelations, and I still had much to learn and experience. I hadn't been the boyfriend to Evelyn that I wanted to be. Probably because, when we met, I wasn't ready to be a boyfriend.

I was now.

She looked up at me, hair stuck to her face, mascara running down her cheeks, a wide-eyed look of awe and fear on her face. No matter what anyone's culture said, she wasn't wilting. She was at the height of her vast, beguiling powers: beauty, intellect, confidence, ability, worldliness. She was interesting, engaging, kind, curious, excitable. Neither commodity nor conquest.

The next wave leapt the railing and as it was about to smash into us, I opened my mouth and screamed, "I love you."

"I love you too," she yelled over the wind, blinking water away as I tried to kiss her. I missed, getting only a mouthful of wet hair. We lowered our heads, closed our eyes, gripped tighter as it tried to blow us from the pole. That's how we stayed, a tangled mess of soaked, cold limbs until, ten minutes later, it was over, the storm blowing down the coast.

We sobbed in each other's arms as fear and disbelief became joy. All around us, people came out of their hiding places, shell-shocked, ashen-faced. *Had this really just happened? And so suddenly?*

Hand in soggy hand, we walked up to the top level of the bridge. It was in disarray—restaurant signs ripped from walls, roofs and awnings collapsed, tables and chairs blown over into the water or swept in piles.

We learned later that it was Istanbul's worst storm in

a decade. A giant wrecking ball that rolled through the city, killing four people, leaving nineteen in critical condition, uprooting one hundred and ninety-two trees, blowing the roofs from thirty-three buildings. Huge hail stones leaving golf-ball-sized holes in cars and smashing windscreens.

We were too late for the dervishes now and so we turned back, picking our way through all the chaos. We'd seen enough whirling for one day. Although, actually, I felt surprisingly calm. Maybe it was knowing we'd come close to the edge yet survived. Or it was another intimacy high, the same I'd felt after we met Leanne, and after we'd made all our confessions on the day when Evelyn had run out of the apartment. We were being honest about something else now, about feelings we'd had for a long time, but in my case, hadn't been ready to acknowledge.

"Just say we did it, hypothetically," I said. "Had a child. How would you imagine that working? And how many do you imagine having?"

She squeezed water from her hair. A simit stall had tipped over and we stepped around a no entry sign on a pole that now lay across the pavement, near a car whose windscreen and passenger window were smashed.

"We could start with one," she said. "See how that goes?"

"Would you want to do that in Berlin, though?"

"Oh God, yes. I mean," she tried to backtrack, "where would *you* want to raise them?"

"I grew up in a small town. Never again. I'd like to give my kid the gift of anonymity."

"There you go," she said, smiling. "Oh, wow." She stopped and pointed. "Look at that." The storm had ripped an enormous tree from its roots, taking power lines with it, smashing two parked cars and tipping over a van. "If someone had been in those," she said. The power lines fizzed.

"Yeah, not that way," I said as we detoured from our usual route up through Galata. "It feels like we're in a post-apocalyptic novel. It's good that we're not, as I have no relevant skills."

"I looked up a spark plug," she said. "Car thing."

"Good to know," I said. We carried on, helping each other over and under debris and hazards. I was both extremely in this moment and pulled back from it, not only somewhere else, but somewhen, in a future it was becoming easier to imagine us sharing.

"I would want fifty-fifty," she said when we were far enough from a car alarm to hear each other again. "As much as possible? Maternity is really generous in Germany. We can split that and we'd almost have enough to live from, without having to work much."

I squeezed her hand. "That could work, yeah."

"You qualify for German citizenship now, right?"

"Yeah."

"Good. I'd like you to get it," she said. We'd given up with pavements and were walking in the road now, too blocked and damaged for the cars and buses to use. "Just in case we end up in some kind of court situation. Like, if we really hate each other one day and have a nasty custody battle? If you're German, you'll have rights I have, and I want you to have them. Just in case."

"That's, wow. Very mature."

She laughed. "I have my moments."

We kept walking—soaked, defiant, in love. I couldn't wait to get back to the apartment. There was something I needed to do.

25

Welcome to Skype
You are now connected to Pete41223
Calling Pete41223
Call disconnected
Calling Pete41223
Line busy
Pete41223 calling ...
Video call established

Mum: Hello, you there, love?

Adam: I'm here.

Mum: Can you hear us? He can't hear us, Pete. Is it working?

Adam: I can hear you just fine.

Dad: I don't think he can hear us.

Adam: I CAN HEAR YOU.

Mum: Can you hear him?

Adam: Your video's switched off.

Dad: How do I turn the stupid bloody thing on?

Adam: The little button with a camera on it, hover and you'll see it. Bottom middle, I think?

Mum: This one, do you think, Pete?

Dad: I don't blooming know, do I?

Mum: Well, click it and see then?

Dad: I don't think we should just click things willy-nilly.

Mum: Oh, shut up and click it.

Camera Activated

Adam: Ah, there you are. One of you. Dad's head's cut off. Can you tilt the iPad up? That's down. No, up. UP.

Mum: He says your head's cut off.

Adam: You don't need to repeat what I say.

Mum: He says I don't need to repeat ... oh, right.

Adam: That's better. I can see you now. How are you doing? Oh no, wait, the video's frozen. No ... it's back.

Mum: Fine, fine. How you doing? Where are you? Are you ... *wet*? What's that in the background? Looks like one of them ... the little fat bald guy? Oh Pete, come on, you know what I mean. Hippies like him.

Dad: Buddha.

Adam: Istanbul. I'm in Istanbul. It's a Buddha thing, yeah. I'm on my roof terrace. There was a big storm. His head fell off. I've just finished taping it back on.

Mum: Poor bugger. Why are you in Istanbul? Is it safe? Actually ... you know ... it's the darnedest thing, but I just read an article about Istanbul. It was about a nice young man, and he met some people in a club and they cut him up and put him in a bin. In pieces. In a bin. I tell ya, there are some right evil buggers around. Don't talk to strangers in clubs.

Adam: I don't go to clubs. I'm thirty-four.

Mum: I know how old you are, you cheeky bugger. You came out of my bloody body, you did. That isn't something you forget, let me tell you.

Dad: You're always bloody somewhere, you are.

Mum: A woman asked me the other day when I was out with the dog about you and I said he lives in Berlin, sort of, but he's never there. Then she asked me what you did, and I said he writes books sometimes, and she said is it anything like that Jojo Moyes, because she loves Jojo Moyes, and so do I, and I said no, not really. It's more about his ... holidays.

Adam: That's nice? How are you doing, Dad?

Dad: Yeah, fine thanks, Ad.

Adam: Work okay?

Dad: Can't complain. See the Chelsea game the other night?

Adam: Must have missed it.

Dad: Lampard's doing a good job, fair play to him.

Adam: Uh-huh.

Mum: What did you want a call for anyway, love? You need money? I can send you some money.

Adam: I'm thirty-*no*, I don't need money. There's someone I want you to meet, actually. Evelyn, come sit down. This is Evelyn, my ... *girlfriend*.

Mum: Oooh, hello, love. I said, didn't I, Pete? I said, I bet he's got a new woman on the go and that's why we've not heard from him.

Evelyn: Hi. It's nice to meet you.

Mum: Evelyn, my love, you are gorgeous. Do you mind if I say that? Well, I've said it now, haven't I?

Adam: We were just in an epic storm.

Mum: I knew it. I told you, didn't I, Pete? It's not safe, Istan-

bul. When are you going to move back to England? Bring Evelyn. Or come visit, at least? So we can meet you properly too, love. And we haven't seen you in ages, Ad. Nan misses you as well. And the dog. We'll have to add you to the family WhatsApp, Evelyn. It's nice here you'll—
Adam: I'll try. *We'll* try.

26

On 17 July 2016, tanks rumbled through the streets of Istanbul and fighter jets flew over the skies of Ankara. Erdoğan was on holiday in Marmaris, while, closer to home, the Chairman of the Joint Chiefs of Staff, Hulusi Akar, was being kidnapped by his own security detail.

A coup. It would be the deadliest in Turkish history. Early into it, Erdoğan took to the TV, urging the fans of both teams, Devout and Secular, to come out together to defend democracy. Thousands did just that. Armed with little more than kitchen implements, they confronted their own army, pulling soldiers from tanks. By the next evening, after three hundred deaths and two thousand injuries, the army had surrendered, and the coup was over.

Exactly who couped—and how much Erdoğan knew about it ahead of time—is disputed to this day. Many in the army claimed they thought it was a military exercise. Erdoğan blamed his enemy, Fethullah Gülen, a powerful yet reclusive cleric, living in the USA. Gülen denies any involvement, and it's likely we'll never know the truth, nor does it really matter. The coup is important because of what it allowed Erdoğan to do, which was to purge all his remaining enemies.

The last day of our trip was the first anniversary of that coup. We were out in what they promised would be a giant day of celebration. "What are they calling today again?" I asked as the Bosphorus Bridge came into view. We were in Kadıköy, on the Anatolian side, crossing off the last restaurant in Evelyn's culinary bucket list.

"Democracy and National Unity Day," Evelyn said, then laughed.

"Subtle."

"I know, right? Good doublespeak, considering what's happened here in the past year on both those fronts. Democracy has taken a real beating."

Thousands were out on the streets in their white commemorative T-shirts, celebrating that Erdoğan was still in charge and that his people—inspired by both their love for both him and Islam—had saved the city.

Or so the legend went ...

"A guy I met at a Couchsurfing event told me the official story has changed a lot," I said. "In the beginning, they said there was a planned attack on Erdoğan's hotel. Then they upgraded that to an attempted bombing. Now the billboards around the city are showing a heroic shoot-out at the hotel between Erdoğan's guards and the insurgents."

"The illustrated ones that look like they're from a graphic novel?"

"Yeah, because weirdly, there's no footage or photos of it."

There would be no shortage of both from this anniversary. A stream of cars passed us, hammering their horns as people hung from their windows, or out their sunroofs, flapping flags and trying to whip those of us on foot, spilling from the crowded pavements, into their chants and songs.

Everyone was out: grandmas in black chadors pushing grandkids in pushchairs—flanked by three generations of their family—talking, laughing, carrying food and ornate tea urns, or picnicking in any small scrap of space left along the shoreline. I did a quick head count: about 80 per cent of the women here were in some sort of headscarf; a disproportionately high percentage for this city, and suggesting not everyone was out and that we were seeing only a certain Istanbuler here—Team Devout.

"It feels kind of like a football game," I said.

She scanned the crowd. "Yeah, but where's the *Away* team? Erdoğan won this match a long time ago. Or, well, a year ago."

After a delicious meal and a pleasant few hours watching the masses, we returned to the harbour and queued for the ferry back. Squashed against its side, as the cool evening wind billowed around us, we looked in awe at the makeover of the city's skyline. Everything was lit up, most buildings wearing the national colours of red and white, or hosting enormous projections of Erdoğan's face.

Honesty had been one of the key themes of this trip. I know that honesty is not a thing you either are or aren't. That you can't always be honest with other people because you aren't being honest with yourself.

Honesty is a process. A commitment to yourself and the important people in your life; that you will try not to be a hypocrite, like Rose's chess genius; bigoted, like Andrea was about refugees and Arabs; delusional, like Hemin's belief communism should get another chance.

And that's why relationships—especially long-lasting ones like Evelyn and I were now trying to build—matter. They help hold you accountable. You have a witness—to what you said, promised, were, at previous points in time.

That was the tragedy of what we were seeing here, on

this anniversary. Turkey had lost control of its national story. No one was left to hold Erdoğan accountable. His opposition had fled, were in prison, or were silenced by fear. Which meant no one was keeping him and his government honest. Pushing back at his very narrow definition of what a good Muslim is, as Oğuz said, and what roles women and minorities can play in public life.

And that couldn't end well. Maybe we were near the end. Maybe there were decades more to come, and if so, I knew they would be intolerant, dishonest decades, full of hypocrisy.

The ferry's engines rumbled to life, and we pulled away from the jetty for the brief trip back to Karaköy. Evelyn put her camera away and wrapped her arms around my waist. "Even if I know the city's flaws now, and there are many, I'll never get bored of that view," she said.

We stopped off on the way home because we had someone to meet. "You got fat, Adam," said a familiar voice as we reached a movie-themed bar near Taksim Square, finding a Kurdish Freddie Mercury impersonator called Hemin quietly lamenting with friends.

We hugged awkwardly, slapping each other on the back. It was strange to see him here, and also in daylight.

"It's her cooking," I said as we took our seats.

"How's Berlin?" I asked.

"Nice to me," he said. "I think. Yes."

"How's it going with the good communist girl?" Evelyn asked.

He puffed out his chest. "Old news."

"Not a good communist?" I asked.

"I guess. In the end? She was, you know, capitalist? But that was not the problem. I am capitalist now too."

"What?" Evelyn asked. "Why?"

He stuck out his tongue. "Age, I guess? There are no

more nice communist girls around. If you want a girl, a family, is ... IMPOSSIBLE."

"But what about your principles?" I asked.

"They are paused, so to say, for now. Capitalism makes me soft." He grabbed at his belly, which didn't look any bigger. "But at a certain age, you must realise you won't win, and give up. Look around, Adam, we lost. This city is lost."

We ordered gintonic—one word here.

"How's it feel to be back?" Evelyn asked. He looked down the narrow street and then back at us. "Today, terrible. Were it not for this wedding, I wouldn't be here. Not during this lie. They destroyed so much of this city already. In some ways it's good to be back, to know that my Istanbul is gone. That Berlin must be my home now."

I got talking to Hemin's friend, a female programmer with thick black glasses and a slight lisp. "Why would you come here now?" she asked.

I nodded at Evelyn. "For her."

"And how was it?"

"It is, was, well, heavy?"

"Ha," she said, laughing. "It used to be heavy. Now it is dead. I will leave soon, like everyone else."

Our drinks arrived. I drifted in and out of the conversation, enjoying the narrow lane, the warm breeze, the feeling of friendship, the simplicity of our daily lives here, thankful for how much time I'd got to spend with Evelyn so early in our relationship until Hemin said, "Peaceful protests, Evelyn, come on." He laughed. "They are not changing anything. You don't agree with me, I know, but it's true." We were back in familiar territory. No matter how much he thought he'd changed, the old Hemin was still there. "I have big news," he said, later in the night, as we were paying our bill.

"You're running for office?" Evelyn guessed.

"No."

"You quit your job?" I tried.

"I wish."

"You're going teetotal?" she said.

His face blanked. "It means you're giving up alcohol," she clarified, and he fake spat on the floor. "This is crazy, this idea. *No.* I'm moving in with my girlfriend."

"You have a girlfriend?" Evelyn asked, confused.

"Yes." *Pause.* "Long time already."

"Hemin." I squinted at him. "A long time hasn't passed."

"Well ..." He shrugged. "She was living in our apartment. So?" The subletter? I'd never met her. Actually, I'd forgotten she existed. "She found a permanent apartment now," he said and grinned. "We will move together. Big adventure, right?" He put his hands together and rubbed. "A family too, maybe? I'm not getting younger."

"When?" Evelyn asked.

"Whenever you can find someone to replace me." He winked at me. "Although I guess you have already?" And I'd thought Evelyn and I were on accelerated timelines. "Come on, Adam." He joked when I said nothing about the idea, positive or negative. "It's time, no?"

"Did I fall asleep and skip a year?" I asked. "What's the rush?"

"Ignore him," she said.

"Love is the great adventure, Adam." He smiled. "Everything else is just politics."

It was a wonderful, intense evening. Politics was there too, given a little space, but then asked to leave. "I have many happy Istanbul memories now," Evelyn said as we arrived at the apartment.

"Me too."

We stopped at our front door. She looked at me,

expecting me to open it, because I always opened it. "Where's your key cord?" she asked.

"I'm not wearing—*hmm*." I had left it and keys at home on purpose. "Do you have yours?" I asked.

"Yes," she said, unzipping, lifting, and rustling around in her bag. "Where is my stupid key? *Grrr*."

"Take your time," I said. "We have time."

27

That night, with Tarlabaşı finally, briefly quiet, I was sleeping contently until someone tapped me politely on the shoulder.

"You awake?" Evelyn asked.

I rolled over, away from her.

Tap, tap, tap. I rolled back over and opened my eyes a crack. She was staring down at me, looking concerned, as if I was about to explode if she cut the wrong wire. "Wot?" I moaned.

"Oh good, you're awake," she said.

"No." I rolled onto my back.

"What if it doesn't work?" she asked.

"Count sheep?"

She put on the bedside lamp. "Not that."

"Too early," I groaned and flapped my arm at her. "No lights." *Was it early? Maybe even so early it was, in fact, still late? Still yesterday?*

"I'm freaking out a bit," she whispered. I removed my mouth guard and rubbed sleep from my eyes but resisted sitting up, and thus committing to whatever this was. It felt like an ambush.

"Can we talk about it in the morning?"

"What if it doesn't work?" she repeated. "We've only ever talked about *if* we want kids. What happens if we try but fail?"

It was no use. I yawned. "But there's," I sat up, arranging some pillows behind me, "IVF and stuff," I said, my voice thick with sleep. "Science is—" I wafted my hand in a way that I hoped suggested *endless*.

Her mouth narrowed. "There will always be something, sure. But what about the cost of that?"

"Financially?"

She was on her knees, her legs tucked underneath her. "Emotionally." She thumped the mattress. "And all that stuff is going to be happening in *my* body. I mean, also to us, sure, but mostly to me. And it could last for years. Cycles and cycles of hope, then despair. Do we want that? Do *I* want that?"

"But we ..." I stammered. "We did all this. I did ..." I gestured around again, vaguely. I still couldn't prepare a Mediterranean salad that wouldn't get laughed out of Italy, but I'd done a lot of growth work. Had revelations and stuff. Drank a lot of disgusting coffee. She had no right to take that away from me. "It's just ..." I sighed. "We agreed one step at a time, no?" I tried to soften my tone. "There was a whole plan. Timelines. Why are you rushing ahead?"

She'd stopped listening. "What if I just *think* I want them because that gynaecologist said I might not be able to have them?" Her voice broke. "Maybe I was so focused on that I've never actually really thought about *if* I want them?" She sobbed, her shoulders slumping. "Or what the cost of actually trying is. For me? For us? There's a real us. I've met your parents."

"Briefly on Skype," I said, but knew that the fastest way to make me want something was to deny me it. I agreed with that. "Didn't you consider all this before you told me your health news?"

She looked away, nibbling her bottom lip, her voice quiet and apologetic. "There was no need," she said. "I knew I didn't want to be a single mum. That I would only do this if I found the right partner. So I focused on that." She pointed a finger at me accusingly. "But then you didn't run away or dump me after all my ultimatums and Death or Glory timelines, like I thought you would. Like any normal person would of."

I beckoned her to me.

She shook her head emphatically. "No."

"Come here."

"Don't distract me," she said as a tear trickled down her cheek.

"I've seen you with them, Evelyn. Heard you talk about them. Dance with them. Coo over them."

She blinked heavily. "So?"

"It's the last night here. You're probably just nervous about going home. About needing to find a job. About Hemin—"

"Hemin is moving out," she said.

"That doesn't mean anything," I said. "Or doesn't have to." But we both knew what it meant, that it was an opportunity to speed up our already hurtling romantic timeline; a chance for more tests, if we wanted them.

"Do you know anyone who has done IVF?" she asked, giving IVF a tone usually reserved for murder.

"You're jump—no," I conceded, after a long sigh. "My friends haven't started having kids yet. Well, only Nick. But he's old."

"Well, I do," she said. "And you've no idea what's coming."

"We've barely started," I said. "We're a long way from IVF."

She wiped the next tear away with the back of her hand. "This is all so heavy," she said. "And it'll only get heavier."

"That's my line."

She squeezed her eyes tightly closed as her crying intensified. I knew this mannerism, how she usually combined it with a howl. I realised how sad it was that I now knew the quirks of her crying.

"I need some time." She sobbed. "When we get back."

"What? Why?"

"There's so much. We're rushing." She looked away and down. "A couple of weeks, maybe?"

Did I need time? I wasn't sure I needed time. Wasn't it supposed to be me who needed time for things?

"O-kay," I said, not sure yet what I actually felt about this.

"We need to be sure," she said. "*I* need to be sure. About me. Not just us."

"We are sure," I said. "About the timelines, anyway. And that's enough, for now."

She gave a brief nod, reached over, and turned off the light. "Thanks," she whispered into the darkness.

28

It was our last hour in the apartment. My suitcase and her backpack were open on the bed. "Can we talk about it?" I asked. "About last night?"

She dumped a clump of her many shoes into the bottom of the backpack. "It was just a wobble."

"It's okay to wobble."

"I know," she said defensively.

"And now?" I asked, as I neatened a pile of shirts to make space for the few things going in that wouldn't be shirts.

"I'm fine," she said, smiling insincerely. "Better than fine."

"Okay," I bent down to pick up the half dozen pesky socks that live and multiply around beds like horny rats. I was sad we were leaving—Berlin would be a place of jobs, obligations, friends, family, careers, taxes, cheese *or* meat sandwiches. A place where we would have to work to pay rent, not a weird, long, heavy holiday.

We said goodbye to the apartment, went next door to the shop, and at Evelyn's insistence, bought two handfuls of ice creams for the neighbourhood kids, thanking them for all the entertainment in a language they didn't understand.

A bus, a plane, a train, a subway, a hug, a peck on the lips, separate apartments. It had just been a blip, I told myself. Understandable, under the circumstances. At home, I got busy unpacking, washing, hanging, and ironing shirts. Here, they had their own hanger, at least.

My apartment felt insufferably quiet without her filling it with her stories and questions, as well as the cacophonous, rowdy, sleep-immune kids of Tarlabaşı screaming and laughing and sledding the day away. Sitting on my couch, listening to birds sing from the top of the giant Linden tree by my window, I reminisced about the people we'd met and the stories we'd heard: Andrea, Abdullah, Sam, Karim, Yezda, Rose, Leanne, and even after some general prodding, Nick. *Why had they all been so keen to tell their story? Why was everyone always so keen to?*

My eyes wandered over to the vanity bookshelf above my desk, the one that contained a copy of all my books. I got up and pulled one out at random, started reading, and catapulted thousands of miles and several years back into my past—in Sulawesi, Indonesia, where I ate biscuits with a dead grandma. I kept reading, captivated by the life depicted in these books, impressed by how much it made sense. How neat it was. How one event led seamlessly to the next—A to B to C and beyond. As every good story should.

Which is not how life works, of course. Just look at Evelyn and me ... we had met randomly in a bar because the only free spot was next to me. A few minutes into our conversation, her friend crashed her bike into a taxi. Again, nothing to do with us. The leg that friend broke created a vacancy for me to fly to India with Evelyn. If she'd had any other viable person to ask, she would have asked them, not me. But she didn't. That trip made an *us*. But inside her body, unbeknown to us both, things were going wrong. Gynaecologist ... Explosive words ... Careers reconsidered ... Timelines accelerate ... Ex-girlfriends get a clandestine interview ... Jobs are quit ... and so on and so on, until we learn Hemin has fallen in love and is moving out.

A rarely leads to B. If we're lucky, it leads to E.

And that's the reason, I decided, as I put the book back in its place on the shelf.

It's only by telling our stories—drunk on champagne in an immigration queue; while slandering on the terrace of our apartment complex in Tarlabaşı; on a hotel rooftop at an event about conflict; over apple shisha with an English-German couple from a cooking course; in the living room of a brand-new home in Diyarbakır—we get to go back and draw in B, C, and D. If we repeat them enough, we can make it neat. We make sense of them, so that we make sense to ourselves and others.

Writing is the same process. Karim was right, as was Sam, Abdullah, Yezda, and Evelyn: writing helps. It's a way to make sense of my story by telling it to a blank page. I'd made the mistake of thinking that writing pulls me out of the moment, when it's the thing giving me permission to really be in it.

Savouring, capturing, and immortalising it.

I stood up, went to my desk, opened my laptop, and let it all pour out. I started in that bar, with the door opening and her entering, my fingers speeding around the keyboard as I tapped furiously, hoping it would untangle the knots in my stomach and the worries in my mind.

I was all-consumed, and it was glorious, and I didn't look up for five hours, and then only to check in with Evelyn. I got out my phone.

Adam: I'm writing. You're going to love your character.
Really fun. Bit odd. Great hair.
Evelyn: That's good.
Adam: You OK?
Evelyn: Yeah. Fine.

I put my phone in the drawer and carried on, spilling out my memory like sand from a bucket. I wrote throughout the night and into the next day as I re-raced through India, dumping all I could remember onto the page. Soon, I was on the plane to Istanbul with her, getting drunk against both our wills.

And all that writing, well, it quietened my demons. For I was no longer messy, real-life me. No, I was Memoir Adam: separate, removed, observable; a protagonist.

He knew what to do. What the story needed for its next chapter. Not its Final Chapter, not The End, not Happy/Happily Ever After, because there is no end (until death) in a life whose only constant is change.

No, this was about what the next chapter should be.

It needed a big gesture, Adam decided.

A surprise.

She liked surprises. She'd said so when they'd done that cooking course. He made some calls. Went and bought boxes. Got busy filling them. Another day passed. Adam spent it the same way, only checking in with her under the guise of asking a question.

Adam: What was the guy called at Chai Talks? The one
that wanted a wife? Ahmed?
Adam: ??
Adam: Abdullah. I remember now.
Adam: This is a lot of silence. Is it awkward?

235

Adam: Hello? Earth to Evelyn?

The next morning, he was just as industrious and just as sure. After a breakfast of peanut butter toast, followed by a lunch of ... peanut butter toast, he went looking for his phone.

Adam: I'm getting worried. You OK?
Adam: This is rude. If you don't answer, I'm coming by.
Adam: I'm coming by. Getting on bike.
Evelyn: No. I'm fine.
Adam: What's going on?
Evelyn: We said we'd take some time.
Adam: You can't not reply.
Evelyn: Sorry. Busy.

He kept writing, and it was a magic that whisked him from his quiet living room back into the deep woods, clinking beer bottles in an illicit bar with Karim, Yezda, Evelyn, and Nick. Then she was waking him from sleep on the last night in Istanbul. As he wrote what he remembered of what she had said—and reflected on the scant, cold messages he'd received since they'd returned—he wondered if maybe everything was less okay than she was claiming?

He closed his laptop; the spell broken for now. The room full of boxes. Not that he owned much. He looked at his desk calendar. Friday. A friend of hers was having a gallery party that night. He knew she'd have to be there to support her, no matter her mental state.

For the first time in three days, he showered, shaved, put on a shirt, and climbed onto his bike. There was just enough evening light to ride without using its lights. Bike lanes, he thought, as he whizzed down one—what a wonderful thing.

In the whole time he'd been in Istanbul, he'd not seen even one. Maybe Germany had swung too far from chaos to order, but right now, it was order he craved.

He reached the gallery: a small space in Kreuzberg, near the Landwehr Canal, soon to become a tattoo studio. This event was its closing party.

Adam: You here? I'm at the gallery now.

People clustered around the makeshift pallet bar, wine glasses and beer bottles in their hands, talking and laughing: about their startups all set to revolutionise how people shared horses; all the times they had drank too much champagne; terrible breakups with liars; wars they had fled; the books and poetry they were reading and writing; their overbearing mothers; their hopes and dreams and why Berlin—where everyone comes to but few come from—was the place that would make them reality.

You know, the stories of their lives, basically.

Into this throng Adam stepped, scanning the crowd for her. He saw someone he knew—a former colleague of hers whose name he couldn't remember. *Robin, maybe?*

He excused his way to her, sliding sideways through the dense throng of bodies of people pretending to appreciate art while hoping to be appreciated themselves.

"Hey," he said, tapping a shoulder.

The person span around. "Adam!"

"Robin!"

"Sara," they corrected.

"Of course," he said, on shuffling feet. There was a DJ. Why was there always a DJ? "Erm ... have you seen Evelyn?"

"Yes. She's ..." they turned back towards the bar, confused. "She was?"

"I think I saw her get on her bike," a man with a narrow hipster moustache said. "Just a minute ago."

He thanked them and excused his way back through the crowd to the street. Holding a lamppost—as if he was about to sing in the rain—he swirled in a circle, looking for her, or her bike. He had been there when she had bought that bike: a stunning, fire-truck red GDR relic that had been in a warehouse for decades. The seller had an entire story about it.

Ah, story. You again ... how funny that the next chapter of their story, the one he'd been able to see so much clearer for the past few days back in his apartment, the reason he'd been packing up that apartment, was already swerving off somewhere new, he sensed, what with her near-ghosting of him and now this, swirling around a lamppost outside a gallery looking for her, sensing that she needed him.

It didn't matter. Whatever the chapter, they'd make sense of it later, together.

He saw her bike ... it was on its side, near some bushes down by the canal, the back wheel spinning slowly. He soon reached it but there was no sign of her as, panicking, he hung over the railing, looking for her in the water.

"Evelyn?" he shouted. "Evelyn?"

Behind him, Adam heard the very distinct, very unpleasant sound of someone forcefully expelling the contents of their guts. He slumped with relief, turned, moved towards the sound and bushes. She was behind them, on her knees, puking.

"It's just me," he said, as he approached gently, not wanting to startle her. He sank to his knees, mimicked her pose, and putting his arm over her shoulder, scooped back some of her hair, half in her face and wet with vomit, as was the front of her green dress.

"Bad time," she said. "And hello."

"What happened?" he asked, trying to project calm again, as he had done in the room with Leanne and her landlord. "Should I call an ambulance?"

"Puking," she said.

"I know, my love."

"Sorry," she said as she lurched forward again as another wave of nausea hit.

He opened her bag and rummaged through its chaos, looking for tissues. "Spinning," she said under her breath as she sat back up. She had been drinking. He could smell it, even through the sick. "Why is it all so spinny? And why are you here? You shouldn't be here. It's nice you're here." Her voice had that up-and-down, roller-coaster quality it always had when she was drunk. You never knew what the speed or volume of any word would be. It was cute and reminded him a little of Hemin. He found tissues. Handed her one. She wiped her mouth, looked around embarrassed as some people passed, probably on their way to the gallery.

"Better," she said.

He helped her up and they sat side by side on a low wall looking at the still canal. Or rather, he sat, and she leaned precariously against him. "I puked," she said. "Sorry."

Adam slipped an arm around her. She let out a long, self-pitying groan. "Did someone spike your drink?" he asked, then noticed how strange it was that this was straight where his mind went. She lifted her head. "I don't think. Did it? Nein. Nein. Cocktails. No dinner. Stupid, Evelyn. Stupid," she said, as if that closed the case. "Why are you here?"

"Later," he said, "we can do all that later. Let's get you home safe first. You're in no condition to bike." He locked her bike up. They hailed a cab. Soon they were passing her large grey door. She didn't notice that he let them in and not with her keys. As he helped her towards her room, they passed Hemin's door. It was open. His room was already empty except for a few posters extolling the virtues of armed resistance.

"I'm messing it up," she said as he flopped her down onto the bed and helped her from her vomit-splattered dress. "Sleep," he said while on his way to her kitchen to get water and a washing-up bowl.

"I don't deserve us," she said, when he returned. He put the bowl on the floor and forced her to drink some water.

"I'm messing it up," she said, letting her head drop onto the pillow.

He sat down on the side of the bed and stroked her back. "You're just drunk. This will be funny in the morning."

She turned her head. "Justine."

"Who?"

"Your friend. I *am* like her."

"Janine?" He guessed, amazed she still remembered that anecdote. It seemed so long since that absurdly intense day that ended on a ferry, where they'd empty their consciences and she'd bravely paraded the skeletons of her closet. "You're not," he said. "I'm available. I'm here."

"Exactly," she said. "It's my turn. And I'm messing it up."

"You're just drunk, honey," he said.

"WHY?" she moaned, turning onto her back. "Uggggh-hhhh. This is horrible."

"Put one foot on the floor."

"Why would I put foot—?" She put one foot on the floor. "Huh," she said with surprised satisfaction. She burped a deep, sickly burp, and he jumped for the bowl, but the nausea passed and so he put it back down.

"I'm messing it up." She closed her eyes. "I am." Her voice was growing distant.

Was she self-sabotaging? Trying to push him away? "I won't let you," he said, standing up and walking to the door to turn off the light. His hand was on the switch when he suddenly saw a connection. Another possibility. "Maybe you wanted to punish your body?"

He waited for an answer. Her breathing had deepened. She'd passed out.

He went home. There was a lot to do.

29

The next morning, a steaming coffee by his side, Adam sat down in his road, trying to keep three adjoining parking spaces empty. The company was supposed to put a thing out. They had not put a thing out. They were a cheap company. Would hiring them be a mistake?

He tried to call them for the sixth time. "Hello?" a man's voice said.

"Hello. It's Adam Fletcher."

"Who?"

"The nine a.m."

"Where? Oh. *Right,*" the man said, begrudgingly accepting that 9 a.m. was a thing.

"It's eleven a.m.," Adam said in a diplomatic voice.

"No one's there?" he asked.

Adam looked up and down the road. "No one is here. When are you coming?"

There was a disconcertingly long pause. "One hour, maybe?"

"What do you mean, maybe ...? *Hello?*"

The line went dead. He needed it to happen today. If it didn't, he was worried he'd change his mind. That his demons would grow louder. Or that she was going to, well, do more of whatever it was she was doing. Finding a removals company on this short notice had been a challenge. Only one was free, and its online reviews were, to say the least, disconcerting.

A car came and tried to park where he was sitting. "Sorry, but there's a moving truck coming," he said to its driver.

"When?" the driver asked.

"Erm, an hour, maybe?"

"What do you mean, maybe?" The driver said, but then reversed and went hunting elsewhere.

An hour passed, somehow, just about. Adam gave up and went to buy pastries. He retook his spot, took out his phone, and made more frantic phone calls.

A van arrived. Six burly men got out, none of which spoke English or German. Their native language—the best he could ascertain—was haste.

"Careful," he shouted, running behind them, checking they weren't breaking his bronze lamp. Evelyn had found that lamp in the back of a thrift store; convinced him he needed it.

A grown-up's lamp.

A writer's lamp.

He might never be the first, but he was the second. Always would be. It was how he contributed, however small, as she had said.

"Slow. Slowly. Hello. *Easy.* No. Stop. Watch out."

They didn't listen, of course, and so began two hours of miscommunication, ever-dwindling trust, and quiet despair, until the van was full and being parked in front of Evelyn's building. Making an exaggerated sad face, and using his fingers, he confirmed again with the men that, yes, it really was the fourth floor, and that he was very sorry about that.

He promised to help them, but first there was just one thing he needed to do.

Quite an important thing, really: he had a girlfriend to surprise and grabbed a box and that lamp, running up the many stairs and letting himself in, using Hemin's key.

Now his key.

"Hey," he said breezily. "Only me. Well, me and half a dozen big surly boys of unknown origin."

She came out of the bedroom dressed in jeans and a white T-shirt, the vomit gone but still deathly pale and looking like she'd both seen a ghost and become a ghost.

"Puke-y," he said, beaming. "I'm moving in!"

"What?" Her nostrils flared. "No!"

He put the box and lamp down and moved towards her. She lifted her hand to keep him back. "What the actual fuck?"

He pushed past that hand and tried to hug her. "Great, right?" he said, but she just stood there, frozen. It was like hugging an irritated boulder. He let go, waiting for her expression to crack from disbelief into warm, gooey joy, but it went the other way instead, from firm surprise to even harder fury.

She crossed her arms. "You can't just move into someone's house."

"It's a surprise. You like surprises."

"Murder is a surprise, but you shouldn't do that either. How did you even get in?"

"Hemin gave me his key." He looked back towards the door. "I thought it would be romantic?"

"Romantic? It's weird. And rushed. And we didn't talk about it. And we should of."

The first two removals men appeared at the front door lugging his desk, tipped at a curious, gravity-defying angle. He'd blocked the hallway with the box and lamp. The man looked at him for instructions, groaning under the weight, out of breath from all the stairs they had ascended, badly, adding several chips and dents to the desk that Adam would only discover later.

Adam pointed quickly towards the living room, the first door on the right, the one place they could put stuff without having to pass down the hallway, past her. He didn't look back at Evelyn, didn't want to know what she was doing. Didn't want to give her the chance to say anything. To send the men away.

"Good. Boss," the man said. They tried to enter the apartment but bumped the edge of the table into the door frame. "Easy! Careful!" Adam shouted then turned back to her.

"You can't do this," she said, baring her teeth.

"The van is downstairs." His hands went limp at his sides. "I've sort of done it, pretty much?"

She flung an arm towards the door. "This is rushed. Take it all back."

He lifted his chin. "You're the one who keeps rushing things."

"Because I have to," she shouted. "We don't have to do *this*." She waved both her arms towards the door now with such a severity he wondered if they'd fly free of their sockets. "It's ..." she looked around, perhaps scanning for viable escape routes, "dramatic," she said, looking from him to the full rack of her many shoes.

Don't run. Don't run. Don't run.

Her back straightened, and she stamped her foot. "Couple meeting," she said. "Right now. Hemin's room." She twisted. "Smells less of vomit," she said as she blustered away from him. He picked up the box and lamp and followed her, noticing now that the lamp was rattling. *Had it rattled before? Should lamps rattle? Perhaps there*

245

was a problem with its spark plug? Oh, no, wait, car thing ...

The room was big, airy, and light. More of all three than he'd known. When Hemin lived here, the door was always closed. He immediately imagined how he would fill it, if she would let him fill it. Saw the perfect spot for his desk. All the books he'd write there. All the sense he'd make.

But that was later. First, he had to explain. In here, at least they'd have some privacy while he did so. She hated awkwardness. She must know that it would be impossibly awkward—even more awkward than them having to return to Psycho Pension with Son and Father—to send these men away again, make them take all this stuff back to *his* fourth-floor apartment.

Had he known that? Relied on it, perhaps? He put the box and lamp down, turned and went and shut the bedroom door. The sounds of men's feet were loud on the stairs, as was the huffing and grunting and shunting and thudding as *his* things entered *her* home. He turned round, then had to step back as she was waving his lamp very, very close to the tip of his nose. "If you annoy me, I'm going to bop you with this."

"It's broken," he said. "I think?"

She lowered the lamp and turned it around in her hands. "Why did you bring a broken lamp? Wait, this is the lamp I found?"

"They broke it. Can you put it down?"

She stared down at it and tried to relax her hands. They would not relax. "Apparently not, no."

He pried it from her and stood it up on the floor as she scowled at him.

"How's the hangover?" he asked.

She clamped her hands to her hips and tilted her head.

246

"What are you doing?" she asked. "Why have you done this?"

His eyes were ablaze with sincerity. Perhaps too much sincerity. "My demons are quiet."

She gave him that same, strange, askance look she'd given him on the bridge, on the first night in Istanbul, when he'd said, *Who am I to judge another man's theatre?*

"I decided we shouldn't move in together," she said, blinking slowly. "We have rushed so much. We didn't need to rush this too. I could have found a new room-mate. It wouldn't have changed our timelines. And, anyway," she shouted, "you can't just move into someone's house!"

He couldn't help but smile. "I beg to differ."

"I also miss the start, you know?" she said in a quieter, sadder voice. "It's not just you."

He reached for her hand. She hit it away.

"We are in the middle, sure," he said. "But it doesn't feel like any other middle I've known. There is nothing average about us, and I don't think there ever will be."

She lowered her head and shoulders, her voice tearful. "I'm fucking it up."

"No, you're not."

There was the sound of glass breaking and they both jumped. It was lucky he had nothing of any actual value, beyond his books and his stories, and the meagre savings they had given him that had allowed him to do all these amazing things with her. The things he would write about to create more savings to do more of those things.

"Where did you find these people?" she asked, her head turned towards the living room, where it sounded like a group of toddlers were ten-pin bowling.

"The depths of the INTERNET," he boomed. "But that's not ..." He sighed. "*Look,*" he said, gesturing back and forth between them, "*this* is more likely to work if it has to.

Let's make it have to. It's okay to be scared. You taught me that. It means you're taking this seriously. We'll never feel ready to have kids. We'll become ready. It's like with my Adulthood Project. You don't just become an adult. It's a process. We'll help each other. Keep each other honest. For a while, we might even be ready. But then the kid will grow and change, and we won't be ready to parent it again. And then we will be. And then we won't be. And then we will be."

"And if there's no kid?" she asked.

"Then there's no kid. Then we'll make *that* a chapter in our story. A few chapters, probably. Look," he said, realising he'd already said look, and that there was no need, because she was looking. She was right there with him, in the room, in the trenches, in the middle.

He wasn't sure what to do with his arms. He lifted them, then lowered them. "I know I wasn't always this certain, but my doubts, they were always about me. I think, because you doubt yourself so much, you can only ever imagine I'm doubting you too." He straightened his back, puffed out his chest. "I have never doubted you. The more I've learned about you, the more I want you. I love you."

It was the first time they'd said it since the bridge. It was clear they both wanted to keep it special.

"I love you too," she said wearily, while looking down at her feet, as if this love was a truth of immense inconvenience. Which it might have been for her, in this moment; it wasn't for him. He moved in, sweeping her up in his arms and nearly knocking her from her feet. "Did you clean your ... forget it," he said and kissed her deeply as a police car's siren screamed past the large windows. Through one, he could see the corner of the balcony where they had sat, in her nook, as she'd given him the non-ultimatum-ultimatum about coming to Istanbul. This was him taking back control, deciding their next chapter. "It has to be now," he said, pulling back just enough that they could look into each other's eyes. Hers were soft now, like usual. "Is that an ultimatum?" she said, laughing.

"Yes." He grinned. "It is. Death or Glory."

It went silent, but comfortably so, as her eyes made a slow circle of her head and she took a long, some might say overly dramatic, drawn-out, tension-building breath.

"Fine," she said. "You can stay. *Idiot*."

The End

* * *

I never planned on becoming a memoirist. Yet, somehow, we're four books into the *Weird Travel* series.

Would you like to know what happened next? The easiest way to show me is to leave a rating, review, or tell a friend about this book. As long as they're selling and people are enjoying them, I'll keep writing.

Thank you for reading,

Adam
PS you can get a free book by joining my mailing list at adam-fletcher.co.uk

ALSO BY ADAM FLETCHER

- Non-fiction -

Don't Go There (Weird Travel Series #1)

Don't Come Back (Weird Travel Series #2 and Writer's Digest Memoir of the year winner)

Tuk-tuk for Two (Weird Travel Series #3)

Lost But Not Least (an exclusive free book for my newsletter subscribers)

Understanding the British

Fast Philosophy

- Fiction (as Adam R. Fletcher) -

The Death of James Jones, sort of

Printed in Great Britain
by Amazon

86467950R00149